Gucci to Goodwill

Debra Vallentyne

PegaWhale

PegaWhale Publishing

First edition, August 2024

This memoir refects the author's own recollections of her
experiences, in her own words. Some details may have been
changed, some timelines and events may have been compressed or
rearranged, and quoted dialogue has been recreated from memory.

ISBN: 978-0-9600029-2-4

10 9 8 7 6 5 4 3 2 1

Editor: Stacy Rice Eldridge
Cover Design and Interior Book Design by Coreen Montagna
Cover image is a photograph of the author taken in Milan, Italy,
by an unknown artist
Back cover photography by Chris Kendig

Printed in the United States of America

With gratitude to
Sheik Ramon Abi-Rached, AKA Ramon Desage,
with whom my wildest dreams came true and I became a Queen.
And when my dreams were shattered,
I became a force.

Chapter One
Cinderella Dreaming

My dream of adventure started as far back as I can remember. I had this unquenchable curiosity to take the road less traveled, to discover a life filled with wonderment and awe, on a journey of unbelievable experiences. Continually immersing myself in books and old movies, wondering why I hadn't been born into royalty, living in a castle, draped with pearls and diamonds. Who was this Cinderella chick anyway? Even though born into poverty, she marries a handsome prince, her true love, and gets to wear all these gorgeous clothes while ruling her magical kingdom. Sounds like something I would love, and I felt that I was just born into the wrong family. Where can I find this elusive prince and this life I deserved? Surely it was my destiny. Savoring stories of glamor and adventure while my reality was looking out at the rain from my tiny second story window in Seattle, I had to get a plan. Gazing over the grayness everywhere in the sky and water, I needed to find a way to create an amazing life with no rules and no regrets. I hated gray. I wanted a life of dragon red, sunshine yellow, mediterranean blue.

My bleak reality growing up in Puget Sound seemed more like Kansas than the Emerald City. I had simply read too many fantasy stories. It was a stretch to say I grew up middle class. We weren't poor either, but my two sisters joked about being on the edge of trailer trash. I think most families are somewhat dysfunctional, and ours was no exception. No one I knew lived in a *Leave it to Beaver* household, nor that fancy house of happiness. I was frustrated growing up, never accepting my station in life. I wanted to rise to the top in life, so I just couldn't accept fitting into a life of mediocrity. Life wasn't fair and someday I knew I would be in those pages of *Town and Country* magazine, smiling to the world.

My mother understood me, knew I was always dreaming of the yellow brick road leading out of Kansas to the Emerald City, the land of Oz in technicolor. Unable to provide me with the life I dreamed of, she was my cheerleader. Better yet, she instilled in me the confidence that I could do anything and the world was mine to conquer, gave me a foundation to chase my dreams. Equally, Mom made our home a place for me and my two sisters to feel safe, protected, and loved while imagining a better future. We always had food on the table and a warm place to sleep, never living in fear we would be homeless. Although it wasn't the luxury life I was dreaming of, she gave me love and security and a platform for my imagination.

My dad was a photographer for the major Seattle newspaper, the *Post Intelligencer*, during the days leading up to the 1962 Seattle World's Fair. Family weekends were spent visiting the fairgrounds watching the Space Needle being built. The Science Pavilion was awesome, learning about space travel and microwave ovens. Dad was an expert at coin toss, winning enormous stuffed animals, giving them to any kid walking by. He met Elvis Presley while he was filming the movie *It Happened at the World's Fair*. He took photos of the Beatles staying at the Edgewater Hotel. My first concert was front row seats watching John, Paul, George, and Ringo performing, "I Want to Hold Your Hand." The entire audience was filled with girls screaming and crying. Dad became quite the local celebrity; he was so good looking. With a charming smile, and a personality able to open any door, I was proud to call him my dad.

A landscape of childhood memories: watching hydroplane races from the shores of Lake Washington; salmon swimming through the boat locks to spawn; weekends driving down the coast and picking clams; picnicking at the base of Mt. Rainier.

My maiden name was Vallentyne, and I was living in a red and white world. Our house was red with white shutters adorned with little carved hearts. Our car was red, as were all the flowers in our big yard where we used to sell lemonade and scream for everyone to vote for Kennedy.

My two grandmothers were seamstresses, and I visited both of them for sewing lessons, learning how to match seams and cut patterns by the time I was twelve, using an old treadle sewing machine you pump with your foot. I was mesmerized by Grandma Mildred's shiny red-lacquered long nails picking up her sewing pins — Chinese dragon red, the same color as her rows and rows of geraniums. Her fitting room was for her society clients where she would drape and fit a dress or tailor a suit. I remember staying overnight in her upstairs bedroom, gazing over the lights reflecting on Lake Union, flashing on and off. Grandma Ruby, living on a farm, taught me how to mend and crochet. When we weren't sewing, I would milk the cow or gather the eggs from the shed out back. I had the best of both worlds: the farm and the city.

Long road trips in our station wagon during the summer months were highlighted by our annual two-week stay at a real western dude ranch. My uncle was the proprietor of the Bar M Ranch near Pendleton, Oregon, on the Umatilla River. It was one of the rare occasions my dad spent holidays with us, riding a horse into the Blue Mountains on overnight camping trips, sleeping under the stars. My sisters and I were responsible for feeding the pigs and milking the cows. There were cowboys playing guitars and marshmallows around the campfire; learning to churn butter; making sourdough pancakes; swimming in the natural hot springs at the edge of the river; fishing for trout. I was never a horse person, but I loved the stars at night and the cowboys with their scruffy boots and hats. It didn't matter that we never went to Disneyland, we had the Ranch.

Summers also meant weekends in the San Juan Islands on a small island called Decatur. It was about thirty minutes from a town called Anacortes, a world away from civilization. Dad dropped us off by speedboat, then returned a month later. Three families vacationing together, but no fathers or husbands, having to fend for ourselves, living in tents. Mom would only feed us if we pumped and carried a bucket of fresh water. Dad, along with the other dads, would show up at the end of the month for drinking and poker. It was on one of the drinking and gambling nights Dad wagered his share of the island that we loved, and sadly, our five years of summertime island living came to an end.

Soon after, Dad lost his job. He was tall and handsome, and knew every martini server in the state. I tried to dance like him when he won the twist contest in Seattle. He loved the ladies and they loved him back, while my mom always looked the other way. His charisma, landed him in hot water. Shortly thereafter, he loaded all of our belongings into the family red Rambler and moved us north, ending up in Anacortes on the road to Canada. A gateway to the San Juan Islands, where all the ferries docked. We rented a fabulous house built in 1880, filled with turn of the century antiques and a piano. It was a three-story white Victorian house, with my bedroom on the top floor—the attic. I had a fabulous view of the ocean through a round porthole window, seeing the boats cruising, listening to the seagulls breaking the morning silence.

I was feeling hopeful, starting high school and making lots of friends. Dad opened up a shop for photography, taking wedding photos and class portraits. Turning fifteen, I knew my parents were having marital trouble. My mom was gaining a lot of weight. Sometimes I wondered why my mom didn't take care of herself, to keep him around. She was so beautiful, reminding me of Ava Gardner with her beguiling smile. Charming all the ladies was Dad's low-hanging fruit, secretly hoping he would leave his martini-loving days in the past. Not a chance.

I needed to earn money if I wanted pizza, bowling, or French fries at the Dairy Queen. I was wanting money for fabric and Vogue patterns. The teenagers in our community picked vegetables and berries outside of Anacortes, buses transporting all of us to the fields. It was the mid-sixties. Radios blaring rock and roll, we worked on our tans and gossiping, while bagging potatoes, cucumbers, flower bulbs. By the end of the summer, we earned $200 each. That was enough for me to pretend I was a dress designer, buying fabric, creating my dreams.

With lofty dreams and needing more money, I acquired a job cleaning the house for this fabulous lady, Emily, who was married to the mayor. She looked like Jacqueline Susanne in *Valley of the Dolls*. Glossy black hair, false eyelashes, and the biggest closet I'd ever seen—flush with fur coats, tall shiny boots, and amazing shoes. Cleaning her house, I just wanted to gaze into her closet. She gave me all her old fashion magazines: *Vogue, Harper's Bazaar,* and *Town and Country*. I love fashion, and studied these magazines like textbooks. I copied the designs from the pages and sewed all my own clothes, wearing outfits like Dior and Gucci in the days of mini-skirts and go-go boots.

And the models. Wow! Richard Avedon was photographing models like Jean Shrimpton and Twiggy, while Verushka was leaping through the pages of *Vogue*. Huge hair, long legs, big jewelry, and glossy lipstick. I sewed a mini-skirt in an hour and spray painted my shoes to match. I was 5' 9" and skinny as a rail, knowing in my heart I had a chance to be one of those exotic girls. I dreamed of traveling to New York, or Paris, and walking in those fashion shows. I practiced my own catwalk saunter, posing like a top model for hours in front of the bathroom mirror. Dad humored me, taking photos of me pretending to be on the cover of a magazine. He'd taken photos of the Beatles, so why not me? My junior year of high school I was invited to model in a fashion show for a local boutique. I taught the other girls how to strut the runway. Could this be my way out of my middle-class existence? Stars were in my eyes and my soul.

I was sharing clothes and optimism with my sisters, Dad was drinking, and Mom was getting fat. We were starting to move into smaller and smaller houses. The world was closing in on us. My sisters and I started to work at my dad's darkroom studio. He would have us sit at the front desk while he ventured to the bar next door. His martini days were far from over, laminating his reputation as the most charming man in town. The ladies, loved him.

It was 1969, I turned sixteen years old and my world was changing. I loved school and was elected class secretary while attending community college at night. It was the days of Basic computers and I was an overachiever, anxious to learn what this new technology was all about. Sex was in the air, and I lost my virginity to the captain of the football team in the back seat of a 1952 Chevy. The car was as old as I was. All my friends asked me what the male genitalia looked like. I was in love with how it looked, how it felt, knowing with my long blond hair and my D-cup breasts I'd probably be seeing a lot more of that in various shapes and forms. Love had nothing to do with it. Sex.

1969 was also the year where the world around me was rapidly changing. Newscasts of the war in Viet Nam, Woodstock, and hippies with their peace signs. I found myself cutting up my Campfire Girl outfits and sewing beads on purple bell bottoms to look like Cher; going to the Led Zeppelin concert in Seattle and smoking pot all summer; driving down the coast to San Francisco to be part of the Haight Ashbury vibe and wearing flowers in our hair. It was such a creative time, with the Rolling Stones and Bob Dylan — feeling like freedom.

Dad was unable to stay out of bars and other women's bedrooms. He was too handsome and too much fun. When Mom blossomed to two hundred fifty pounds, he left us. Packed up and moved out, in no time having a new girlfriend; cute, sexy, spunky. From a man's point of view, I could see why he fell for her. What I couldn't understand, though, was how he could leave his three kids. Maybe this domestic life of a wife and family just wasn't for him. I was the oldest of my sisters, having been my mom's confidant for years. I was the shoulder to lean on, and she was a wreck, having no skills, no work experience, no husband and three kids to support.

Dad left us no money and a pile of bills. I tried to connect with him while visiting the lakeside cabin, he moved into. He didn't know where his future would take him, but he was so unhappy in his marriage, staying was not an option. There was neither talk of reconciliation, nor guilt over leaving his family. I understood his longing for freedom, but as his daughter I felt abandoned. We smoked a joint and said goodbye, knowing we were both on our separate paths. My loyalty was with my mom. It wasn't an argument, a parting of ways. Mom needed me. My dad was on another path. Selfish.

The shit hit the fan. My mom and I talked for hours about our options. Her first choice: driving off a cliff. I was shocked she said that.

"Mom, don't be so selfish! We are all in this together and we will figure it out."

Advice from my sixteen years of life experience. Hugging and crying, knowing we had each other's back. In no time, Mom packed up her three daughters and driving us out of town.

We drove straight to Aunt Mary's two-bedroom apartment in Bellevue, Washington. Aunt Mary shared a bedroom with my mom, my two sisters the other bedroom, and I slept on the sofa in the living room with my cousin Don. Mom received welfare and food stamps, and eventually was hired by the welfare office. We lived on powdered eggs and peanut butter for a year. All of us gained weight. Mom found a diet doctor who prescribed white crisscross amphetamines. It was totally legal in those days. I lost twenty pounds. Mom lost one hundred.

My sisters and I painted the other apartments in the complex for rent reduction, quickly learning to tape, trim, and roll-out a two-bedroom apartment in a day. My very chic and fashionable Aunt Mary paid me to make her an entire new wardrobe. We were going to somehow make ends meet and always stayed optimistic. Organically we banded together in order to survive. Rent was paid.

Not yet graduating from high school, I earned quite a few college credits at night, allowing me to enroll at a community college in Seattle. My desire to become a model was unwavering, but I was pulled by the field of genetics, DNA. I'm not sure what I was thinking. It was a feeling. Trust.

Looking back, these difficult times gave me the drive to succeed. Mom instilling that we can accomplish anything — keep moving forward and have a back-up plan. Always pay the rent first.

Moving out at seventeen, I hoped to create more space at the apartment. I spent a year sleeping on the sofa in the living-room. I desired to see the world outside of Seattle, to explore if the grass was greener on the other side.

My boyfriend at the time and I painted my grandparents' house for two thousand dollars, launching us on a cross-country road trip in his lime green 1969 Dodge Charger. We landed in Washington, DC, where I spent six months selling clothes in a boutique where all the clients were African-American and I was the only white chick. Marvin Gaye and Dianna Ross played in the background. Hot pants and wigs were worn in those days. My new girlfriends insisted I adorn an enormous afro, wanting me to be one of them, welcoming me into their culture. I was having so much fun!

It was too cold for me in the winter, so my boyfriend and I cruised down the east coast to Ft. Lauderdale, Florida, toward the sun. I worked as an aerobics instructor at Vic Tanny's Health Spa and sold Mary Kay cosmetics on the side, hoping to sell enough creams in the pink jars to earn a pink car, maybe even a Cadillac convertible. Cruising Palm Beach with the top down wearing huge sunglasses, I wanted to be glamorous. Never happening, but I was now in Florida living in bikinis and listening to Cat Stevens playing guitar on the beach.

Not long after landing in Florida, I broke up with my boyfriend. I was not yet eighteen. My option was a Motel 6 when it was six dollars a night. I hadn't seen enough of the world and going home to the sofa with Aunt Mary wasn't an option. First day at the pool, I met a gorgeous college student who went to Kent State. She was a witness to the campus uprising a month earlier when a group of protestors were fired upon by the National Guard. These were such radical times in the early seventies with the Viet-Nam war and Jane Fonda filling our TVs. My new friend's professor boyfriend from North Carolina recently rented a sailing yacht.

"Do you know how to cook? We need an onboard chef."

Easy answer. I said yes, imagining a summer of glorious yachting.

The following day, I checked out of Motel 6 and headed down to the dock. On a Nathaniel Herreshoff sailing vessel with a crew of three girls and six male college students, Captain Buck was taking us to the Bahamas! It was time to start planning menus for a two-month cruise heading south. My sailing days in Anacortes were bearing fruit, never feeling seasick, loving the ocean — setting sail with the wind at our back and the sun in our face.

We sailed from Ft. Lauderdale to the Bahamas in three days. Two of the men spent the entire trip throwing-up and the captain spent his time with a girl in his stateroom, leaving me and my new girlfriend cooking and cleaning while the crew caught fish for dinner. Entering the port of Nassau, I was awestruck by the yachts and the casino looming in the distance. I lost my last two hundred dollars in cash the first night in the casino. My island adventure began.

The next month we ported all the islands in the Bahamas, stopping almost daily for a walk on the beach or a trip to a simple restaurant. We ate fresh conch and exotic colored fish, picked ripe mangoes from the trees. Steel drums played at each stop. My chef skills were getting honed. The whole experience — magical.

Next stop, Jamaica, docking in Port Antonio. Rats jumped on and off our boat, scurrying around our galley looking for food.

My girlfriend and I jumped ship for the day, wandering around town acting like tourists, discovering rum raisin ice cream. We stumbled upon a magnificent park where live music was playing, where we were invited to join a group of guys with dreadlocks and guitars. One of the guys named Bob played cutting edge music on his guitar to his circle of friends. A huge joint passed around the circle and Bob Marley handed it to me. Taking a deep drag, I then passed it on. A circle of peace and love with everyone elevating their consciousness.

His music and vibe would soon change the world forever, changing me forever. An afternoon delights.

Captain Buck was busy making a trip to Ocho Rios. He was looking into buying large quantities of cannabis for our return trip. Now apparent, I was caught up in a dope run in the summer of 1971. Well, the price was too high in Jamaica, or maybe he just didn't score, so we were off to Haiti.

We docked next to an enormous cruise ship in Port au Prince, and Captain Buck was off and running to find his supplier. We were exploring the town, looking for a small cafe when I met someone connected to Jean-Claude Duvalier inviting me to dinner at a beautiful restaurant. After dinner, drinks. We passed through curtains of beads into the back garden where we could hear chants of voodoo. We sat at a wonderful table with lots of rum. The next day, he visited the boat and gave me a bottle of Dior nail lacquer. It seemed like a huge luxury at the time.

Captain Buck scored his supply of cannabis. After dark, six extra-large jib bags, the canvas bags used to store sails on a sailboat, were loaded on board. They were so big they would only fit on the floor of the galley or between the bunks. We were in Haiti and needed at least a week to get back to Florida. How was I going to cook? We took turns sleeping on mounds of cannabis and sitting on the upper deck in the hot sun. We were all a little on edge and paranoid we would get caught. The boat was powered by a very small motor and at times with no wind, we would be drifting for hours. Drifting along the coast of Cuba, at times we saw the US Coast Guard vessels on patrol. I hoped we wouldn't get busted, never being on a dope run before.

Our luck was changing. The wind picked-up, and we sailed into Key West, dropping anchor two hundred feet from shore. Night fell, lights flickering from shore, and a small speedboat cruised out to meet us. The cargo was transferred and we headed back to Ft. Lauderdale where we got dumped off at the docks.

With no money and no job, it was time to call Mom for a plane ticket home. She would set me straight and put me on a path to greatness. I called her from the pay phone, knowing she would accept the charges.

Chapter Two

Catwalks, Cameras, and Playboys

Mom — she bailed me out so many times I couldn't count. This time it was a plane ticket home from an adventure at sea, but sometimes it was as simple as twenty bucks to get me through the week. I was her oldest, her favorite and her dreams for me were bigger than my own. I brought joy into her life and she brought unconditional love.

Tanned and toned from weeks on the boat, I knew I was cute enough to strut the catwalks. It had been my dream since slipping on those Gogo boots.

Confidently walking into John Robert Powers Modeling School in downtown Seattle, signing up for the beginner course. I figured this was my best option, pursuing a career and finding a way out of Seattle. I learned how to apply my own make-up and put together a more professional sense of fashion. Just looking at magazines wasn't enough. The school introduced me to hair stylists and photographers and taught me how to book a job through their agency.

Attending school two days a week was pretty expensive. I had to find a way to pay for my new career choice. Working out of my dining room, I learned how to knot macrame, creating these enormous wall hangings. Building a display booth, touring art fairs selling my goods on weekends and throughout the summer. My business was growing, and I ended up selling hanging planters wholesale to World Market in San Francisco. Macrame Queen of the West. Hustle.

At school I perfected my walk for fashion shows at retail stores like Nordstrom, I. Magnin and Frederick and Nelson. They were the best during the seventies. The clothes were fabulous — make-up artists painting your face and audiences staring-up at you. The highest of stilettos, the flair of fur capes across your shoulders, taunting the front row with a smile. I was dressed in designer gowns and jewels one day and the next spray tanned for bikinis. Each fashion show had a fitting, a rehearsal, and one or more catwalk presentations. Sometimes the clothes changed so fast we would layer the outfits, stripping off the outermost layer for the next presentation. It was a world of chaos, confusion, and glamour. I Love it.

The school hired me to teach classes, allowing me to be downtown every day and involved in the whirlwind of fashion. The school was located directly on top of a little coffee shop called Starbucks on Pike Street. One of the other teachers, Margie, and I used to talk to the owner, Howard, about his dream of expanding his coffee shop. Margie was fabulous, flaming red hair, avant-garde clothes, and smoldering eyes — reminding me of both Cher and Diana Ross. I was her opposite, an elegant, chic, blue-eyed statuesque blonde. We both were very serious about school, determined to make history in fashion. Our students would hang out downstairs listening to Howard and testing all these exotic coffees. With so many models in the shop, the place was jammed with customers. The place to be seen in downtown Seattle.

Working as a model was an introduction to society, meeting anybody and everybody. Leslie Wexner was in Seattle for his line of stores called the Limited, and later Victoria's Secret. Bill Gates was starting Microsoft, and I dated a handsome Greek named Vassily Vyzus. Vassily would go on to become a prominent real estate developer. I also dated a man named Paul who had a sixty-foot Hatteras yacht and an apartment in San Francisco. I was now almost twenty-one years old, learning about art, culture, lobster, and champagne. A far cry from the days of powdered eggs. Paul liked jazz and oysters and took me to the best restaurants in Seattle. My favorite was Canlis with a view overlooking Lake Union. I really, really liked champagne!

Catalog print work was plentiful, and I did quite a bit of work for ski-wear manufacturers like Sportscaster and Eddie Bauer. The companies paid all expenses when there was a fashion show out of town. I was starting to realize my dream and was grateful for finally being on the right path. Thank you, Mom, for having my back.

I decided to splurge a little. Finally making some money, I bought myself a new Datsun 280Z. It was my first car. I felt so lucky—having lots of work, wonderful clothes and dating some pretty amazing men. Front row tickets to Elton John, Led Zeppelin, and Bette Midler. Paul used to take me cruising across the lake to the University of Washington football games where we tailgated on his yacht. He was definitely my most serious boyfriend at the time, but I was young and my dreams were bigger than Seattle. I wanted more.

My girlfriend Theresa Morelli and I were doing catalog work together for a ski wear manufacturer when she booked a gig in Milan. She called me a couple weeks later describing the wonderful time she was having and making lots of money. She was in need of a roommate and missed me. How soon could I fly out? I hopped on a plane three days later, landing in the center of fashion. Italy!

My first day, I went up to the roof of our hotel, the Principessa Clotilde, to bask in the sun. The model next to me was wearing a tiny white bikini, looking about eight months pregnant. She was German and we chatted for hours. She had married into a fashion empire. Did I need a job?

Blessings or coincidence? Didn't matter.

The following day, a car picked me up at the hotel and whisked me to the Italian countryside, where I met the owners of the factory and their young designer named Gianni. The pregnant girl from the roof was there, introducing me to everyone. Touring the factory, meeting the seamstresses and the other models. As I had the perfect measurements for a fitting model, they hired me on the spot. The next day, returning to my new job at a high fashion design studio in Italy, I could only pinch myself. I was going to work with Gianni Versace.

The car picked me up every day and we would drive to the atelier. We wore black ballet leotards while the designer draped fabric on us. Gianni preferred live models over sewing forms so he could see how the garment moved. I would be draped in a design then move to the seamstress who would remove the garment and sew the first idea, then return to the designer for alterations or adjustments. A few fittings later Haute Couture was ready for the catwalk and a top photographer like Herb Ritts would photograph the finished design. Gianni was a perfectionist, wanting every detail to remain how he had envisioned it. Never talking much, he was polite and appreciative of all the people around him that were working through his creative process.

When not working as a live model I would book jobs working for catalogs, magazine photos, or runway shows. I was represented by an agency in Milan that would take care of the bookings for interviews, fittings and scheduling the actual shows, arranging transportation to get us to our work, and making sure we were paid. I ran into some of the top models of the time, like Jerry Hall, who was my absolute idol. She was dating Mick Jagger at the time and I was in awe.

Theresa and I were always invited to the best nightclubs and restaurants. My favorite was Nepentha where all the models used to hang out and where I met the fashion agent, Wilhelmina, who was visiting from New York. Weekend lunches were spent outside the city in opulent country estates. We were dating wealthy playboys, drinking champagne. Dressing scantily to show off our long legs while dancing to the sounds of the disco queens. Cocaine was everywhere and free. It was wild, fun, and everything you read about in the gossip magazines. We were models living in Milan. It was a way of life.

We stayed at Principessa Clotilde Hotel, or more scandalously known as the Princess Clitoris—two-hundred and twenty rooms filled with models and actresses waiting to be discovered. I was one of them. The wealthy playboys stalked and hunted us down while lounging in our lobby, inheriting fortunes from their families with all the time in the world to lure any of us into their net. Everyone was sleeping with everyone. Some girls were taken advantage of and passed around. Some girls married their suitors, and some, like me, were given a glimpse into the homes and bedrooms of the super-rich. It was a taste of opulence, decadence, and all-night sex. Waking up on silk sheets, under a seventeenth century tapestry, with the maid tapping on your door carrying a tray of breakfast. A brief exotic interlude, before real life returns.

I dated Umberto Caproni, heir to the Caproni Aviation fortune, who had a private museum at his country estate filled with antique bi-planes and horse drawn carriages. His villa walls were lined with mirrors and master paintings from the Renaissance. He would pick me up in his Porsche and we would speed away to this weekend retreat near Trento or to his townhouse inside Milan. At the townhouse, we sat in the breakfast room, looking at his pond filled with black swans. With him, I discovered a life of maids, chauffeurs, and frivolous wealth.

I also dated Flavio Briatore—a billionaire who would later become the boyfriend and baby-daddy of Heidi Klum—spending a weekend of sex and shopping in Venice at the Hotel Danieli. My roommate Theresa's boyfriend, Lamberto, was Flavio's best friend, so we frequently double dated, taking speed boats from Venice to a small island to see the Murano glass factory, spending hours watching them make those enormous chandeliers. Lamberto later married Theresa, living wonderful years in Italy with the love of her life. She was one of the lucky ones, finding her prince charming.

After a year of working in Italy, I returned home to Seattle, reflecting on how much I've grown and changed. I felt so international and sophisticated. Like I didn't belong in Seattle, anymore.

Margie was working at I. Magnin as a buyer, and I met her for coffee at the Starbucks on 5th and Pike.

I was only back for a short time, having bookings back in Milan in a few days. I decided to sell my Datsun 280z, buying a fabulous long-haired sable fur coat. It made more sense than my car. I felt a bit like Jack and the Beanstalk, trading my gorgeous car for a handful of beans.

When returning back to Milan, I found my own apartment. I was now dating one of the sons from the Italian family that owned the atelier where I worked. I brought back from Seattle a twenty-pound salmon, chilling it on dry ice—a gift for my friends who have everything.

Gianni was invited for dinner, along with his brother Santos, and I was cooking. I knew how to cook a fish. Gathering in the enormous kitchen at the family estate along with the two Versace brothers, we were all drinking wine from the estate cellars, offering each other cooking tips, while I prepared the fish and they cooked the pasta. No staff was on hand that night to witness our frivolity. Dinner was served outside in the gardens amidst flowers, laughter and Italian hand gesturing. An intimate setting. I had learned enough Italian by this point to at least laugh at the jokes, though everyone was doing their best to speak English. Grating fresh parmesan cheese over the pasta, pouring more wine. For dessert, Asti Spumante and lemon gelato. Heaven.

I felt like I was growing into this world and appreciating every moment with this family. They had a villa on the island of Sardinia, and I spent two summers with them laughing, cooking, and sailing. Taking karate lessons, driving around Sardinia discovering boutiques in Porto Cuervo and white sand beaches next to the Hotel Cala di Volpe. Cruising to Portofino or Genoa, meandering around the tiny ports looking for cafes with the freshest fish or cioppino.

These times in Italy forever gave me a glimpse into life at the top: learning about fashion, art and architecture; attending operas, symphonies and experiencing European life. I was walking through the doors of my Cinderella stories.

I was always living my life from the unorthodox perspective of putting myself in the place I want to be and waiting for the world to catch up. I was not born with a silver spoon in my mouth nor into high society, not even middle-class. I learned that being beautiful can open many doors, but you better be able to open your mouth and be charming or smart or that same door could close. I really did have a champagne taste and a beer budget. So, I just put myself in life situations and let opportunity knock. Be the person you want to be, and you become that person. I was finally becoming the person I dreamed of. Maybe it's a bit like acting, but who knows the difference?

After two years in Italy, I was getting homesick for my family, missing my mom and my sisters. I had learned to speak Italian and mastered the catwalk. All the opulence and glamor of Europe gave me an education into life at the top, but I hadn't found my soulmate. I'd dated men who inherited fortunes and only knew how to spend money. Some were under-educated and started to sell the family paintings to pay for their grand estate maintenance. Rarely did I have a conversation with an entrepreneur or visionary. I did not see my future being a kept woman in a foreign country far away from my family. Living the past two years was a fairy tale, but I was wanting reality, family. I wasn't so sure the rolling hills of Italy was my destiny.

At twenty-six, I knew my modeling days were waning. These were the days when models were cast as either runway or print. I was working predominantly as a runway model, occasionally taking jobs for catalogs and magazines. Gianni was now going to focus on his own brand which would launch him into super stardom. He was working with famous print models like Linda Evangelista and Stephanie Seymor, definitely much younger and more famous than I. Cable television was launching MTV, and Fashion TV made Naomi Campbell, Cindy Crawford, and Claudia Schiffer into stars.

I was going to take a break from the fashion world and go visit my family. This time I did not need to ask Mom for a plane ticket home.

Chapter Three

Yachts and Fishing Vessels

I flew Alitalia back to Seattle, Mom picking me up. She remarried several years back and I hadn't seen her or my two sisters in two years. Margie was living in a cute cottage in West Seattle where I visited, drinking vodka tonics, listening to Patsy Cline and Frank Sinatra. I'd heard nothing but Italian disco for two years and this music was a reminder I'd been gone too long, had so much to catch up on. Both my sisters were now married; I missed the weddings. Missed all the small things, like sister chats over coffee and taking my mom out to lunch. My intention on this return trip was to visit for a couple weeks, as I still had bookings back in Milan. I felt so worldly sitting with my sisters. I had grown into a sophisticated fashionista at last. They were so happy and content in their newly married lives. Was I missing something?

My old boyfriend Paul reached out, wanting to take me to dinner. He mentioned his new yacht, wanting to show it to me with a Lake Union cruise and cocktails. Just like old times. Dinner at Daniel's Broiler for lobster and champagne, surprising me with a marriage proposal. Knowing Paul for six years, he was familiar. My years in Italy made his heart grow fonder, and he promised he would treat me well. I was missing my mom, my sisters, and my girlfriend Margie.

I said yes, hoping I wasn't being too spontaneous. Perhaps, I was homesick or maybe I was ready to stop running at full speed living life at the top. Perhaps, I was wanting to get married and discover what having a partner is all about. I'd never been in a long-term relationship lasting more than three months. Hopefully, I was about to enter a world of domestic bliss.

Paul was a food broker representing SaraLee, Heinz, Alpo, and Rice-a-Roni amongst other brands. He dealt directly with the Heinz family and Mark DeDomenico at Rice-a-Roni. His beautiful yacht, a tool to entertain clients. We quickly settled on a two-story home in downtown Bellevue, only a short walk to the yacht club on Meydenbauer Bay, furnishing the house and getting married in our backyard with family and a few friends. My single girl days were over. Marriage was a new path to explore, and I wasn't sure I had chosen it correctly. The wedding ceremony was not what I had dreamed of, but my sisters were with me and I was surrounded by love.

Married to Paul, I became the hostess serving charcuterie to his clients on the aft deck. Spending most evenings offering cocktails, cruising Lake Washington until it was time to dock at a lakeside restaurant. Tying up the boat and taking our guests for fresh seafood from Puget Sound. Seattle is famous for oysters, crab, and salmon. Paul was an expert boat handler, and I was an expert at enjoying the cruise. Weekends we would go through the Hiram Chittendom locks and cruise up to one of the San Juan Islands, putting out crab pots or fishing for cod from our Boston Whaler. My favorite spot was Roche Harbor on San Juan Island, eating oysters. On occasion meeting up with other boat owners for clam bakes, wine, and margaritas. It was simple, yet decadent.

Paul was sixteen years older, having been married before with four children. His children were not much younger than I, resenting our marriage. Not to mention jealous of my experiences in Italy. I found it difficult to build a life with him with so much negativity. He had a vasectomy and didn't want any more children. Paul was a nice guy but didn't dream of the same future as I did. Happy with the status quo. I felt my days passing by too quickly serving cocktails. He didn't want me to work, therefore I would never have either a career or children. Would my future be without merit? I needed something to fulfill my creative spirit and occupy my days.

Modeling was not an option — twenty-eight was too old for the runway and I didn't want to return to teaching. I enrolled in Interior

Design school so I could keep my love for visual beauty, but focus on homes rather than fashion. Our home was in need of a makeover, and I relished in the thought of creating a lifestyle ambience for my husband and a great place to entertain. Analyzing my life, I felt this was a perfect solution for me and my life with Paul. Decorating our homes and perhaps even growing a lifestyle business.

I surprised my husband with the news I was going back to school part time to study something I loved.

Rather than be supportive, he exclaimed, "Why would you do that? You will become educated and then divorce me."

I was at a loss for words. I couldn't stay married to a man wanting to keep me uneducated and childless. A recipe for disaster. I needed to grow, to dream, to get excited about a new venture. I couldn't do it with a husband wanting to keep me in the dark about life itself. He gave an order, demanding I stop this crazy idea of becoming an interior designer. No compromise. He agreed to a divorce.

Our marriage lasted two years and I was now enrolled in the American Academy of Interior Design. Loving school, loving the design field, and loving my future. Never was there a discussion on what could save our marriage. We were getting divorced and my dreams of happily ever after vanished. Six months later, I used my divorce settlement to buy out the owners of the design school, asking my sister Shannon to run it with me, imagining a school centered around students dreaming of their future in an exciting world of design.

I'm more creative and my sister is very technical. Within a year the school was accredited, graduating hundreds of students. We moved the school from Capitol Hill to downtown Seattle next to the Pike Place Market and my favorite Starbucks coffee shop. We knew all the designers and furniture manufacturers in the Pacific Northwest. I started dating again. Mostly architects. Dreams of a life with fabulous homes and vacations centered around architecture filled my head. Graduation ceremonies at the Seattle Design Center were my first attempts at public speaking. Our alumni were working as designers, architects, window display artists, and furniture representatives. Shannon and I were truly proud of what we created. The best part was we did it together. Sisters.

I was still close to some of my friends from Anacortes, having spent my high school years there. There was a large population of Yugoslavian immigrants in Skagit County involved in the fishing industry. Most of them kept their hundred-foot boats in Anacortes and sailed them north to Alaska to fish for king crab or salmon. My high school boyfriend, Tony Franulovich, had his salmon boat docked in Seattle for repairs. He was always calling to meet me for a drink on Lake Union, for old times' sake. We had stayed friends all these years.

It was a Friday afternoon and Tony called to see if I was interested in meeting him at the docks for a drink. Arriving at the boat, I climbed onboard, yelling Tony's name. I was familiar with boats, so I checked out the galley and the pilothouse. No answer. I turned around to a vision. A tall, dark, handsome man who was also looking for Tony. Terry was his name, picking up the slack and taking me out for a drink. Terry was an Anacortes native, a crab fisherman working out of Kodiak.

We had a lot in common. Terry loved champagne and lobster as much as I. Turns out Tony owed Terry money and Terry had come to collect it. Big mistake. Terry thought I was the best thing he'd ever seen and sent me flowers every day. Delivering cases of king crab and bottles of Cristal champagne to my apartment overlooking downtown Seattle. Picking me up in his Mercedes convertible, riding around town with the Rolling Stones blaring. Terry was such a breath of fresh air after my marriage to Paul. Paul was steadfast and serious; Terry was wild and crazy. He made me laugh until I cried. Our romance lasted a couple months before he had to take his boat back to Kodiak. Crab season was approaching and there was money to be made.

Would I like to join him in Alaska? Why not.

A few weeks later I was on a flight to Anchorage, then to Kodiak on a little puddle jumper airplane. Wearing my Sable fur coat knowing it would be freezing. Terry was there waiting to meet me in the rugged town of Kodiak. I walked through streets of mud, overdressed for the taverns and pool halls down at the docks. Arriving at his one-hundred twenty-foot boat, he lifted me on deck. Enormous square crab pots were stacked four or five high on the aft deck and the crew was waiting to cast off. We headed out to sea in calm waters as the sun set, while I sat next to Terry in the captain's chair of the wheelhouse. Music was blaring and the crew was in a jubilant mood.

As the sky turned pitch black, we headed northwest toward Russia. I could see other vessels far off in the distance pitching up and down in a dance with the sea. The next day, we arrived at a spot

Terry determined was the fishing grounds for this journey. The crew started dropping pots overboard with a steel motorized winch. Each pot had a large orange floater with a number painted on that was attached by a nylon line. Over fifty pots went over the rail. The sea was getting rough.

Terry marked all the pots with a GPS locator and in no-time we headed back to the first pots dropped. A time span of twenty-four hours from being dropped and then hoisted back-up. The pots were bursting with king crab. The winch grabbed the pot, swung it onboard, and dumped the crab into the hold below. After every pot was unloaded, the process was repeated, hoping the fishing grounds were plentiful.

The seas were getting rougher, perhaps thirty-foot swells. The boat was throttling up and down all the time the crew was picking the pots. No one on deck was talking except for simple commands to keep the deck safe. Terry spoke through a loudspeaker from the captain's wheelhouse to keep everyone synchronized. This routine lasted twenty-four hours per day for an entire week. Finally, the tanks were filled to the brim and we turned the boat around, heading back to Kodiak. A half-million dollars' worth of crab in the tanks.

We celebrate by going to the pool hall and ordering lobster and champagne for the entire crew. Kodiak was brimming with hundreds of drunk and rowdy fishermen celebrating making big money in the two-month season. Pool halls were full, music was loud, and all the men needed a bath. I'd been at sea for a week and it was time to get back to Seattle and the design school. Terry was heading out for another few weeks of crabbing, but I'd had enough. I couldn't wait for him to get back to Seattle.

The crab season flew by and Terry was back in Seattle celebrating a profitable season. While in port he was approached by Glenn Bell, the founder of Taco Bell.

"Would you be interested in captaining a new boat operating out of Honolulu to fish for shrimp?"

Taco Bell was adding a new item to their menu and wanted to supply their hundreds of restaurants. Terry, wanting a change, jumped at the idea of warm weather fishing. I was happy he would be in Seattle for a couple months preparing the vessel for the long voyage across the Pacific. He was busy working on the boat and Shannon and I spent time together enrolling another semester of students.

The trip would take approximately two weeks to cross the Pacific with a crew of six, picking up two more crew in Honolulu. Shannon and I were doing well at the school, but enrollment was a bit down as Seattle was feeling an economic slump. Terry invited me on the two-week crossing. Shannon encouraged me to go, so I packed my bags for Honolulu. I was feeling like another adventure, sailing across the Pacific would suffice. I'd be back in a month's time.

We left at dawn, cruising a direct route across the Pacific with no land in sight. Spending time listening to music, eating, and sleeping. Everyone on board shared the responsibility of being on watch for a four-hour shift, including me. I had to be taught radar, radio, navigation, and how to avoid oncoming ships or obstacles in the sea. Most importantly, I was taught to alert the crew if we were getting into danger. We hadn't seen vessels or birds in two weeks, only the open ocean. Flocks of albatross and seagulls started appearing over the boat and we knew land was close. The sea was a beautiful deep blue and the weather warm, having changed from fifty-five degrees in Seattle to ninety degrees approaching Honolulu. Everyone changed into shorts and flip-flops prior to stepping off the boat.

Arriving in Honolulu, we met with the Taco Bell representatives who approved all the expenses for the shrimp boat. I talked to Shannon and all was great with the school, and I asked if she was okay with me spending a couple more weeks in the Pacific? Terry was going to fish for shrimp in the Hawaiian Islands on the furthest western point of the Pacific, close to the Marianna Straight. I was going to be the only woman aboard. Oh, one more thing, did I know how to cook? My cooking skills would come in handy.

It was a long cruise to the fishing grounds. We left Honolulu heading due west, passing all the Hawaiian Islands toward the Northern Marianas. It was so beautiful. Blue skies, albatross flying overhead. The color of the water changed from blue to turquoise, to deep navy blue, and then black at night. It was necessary to have several guns on board, including an automatic machine gun, for security. A commercial vessel fully loaded with equipment and supplies was a prime target for modern day pirates. We needed to be aware and prepared.

We cruised for nearly a week, arriving at waters so clear you could actually see the schools of shrimp swimming below the boat. Shrimping proved difficult, and we were searching continually for better grounds. Where were these massive amounts of shrimp Taco Bell was planning to put on their menu? We communicated frequently with the main office in Honolulu and everyone was beginning to wonder if this had been a good idea. I was getting anxious, wanting to get back to dry land. I wondered if this was going to be my future—a cook on a shrimp boat. Arriving back in port, Taco Bell decided they wanted to refit the vessel from shrimping to lobstering. It would be a quick ten-day turnaround, so I spoke to Shannon frequently. Our enrollment was up and we had classes starting in thirty days. All was great in Seattle, so I would take one more trip out, this time fishing for lobster.

Lobster fishing grounds were a lot farther west in the Marianas Islands near Guam. It was a ten-day trip before we threw any lobster pots overboard. In the middle of these islands the water can get so shallow you have to be careful not to run aground. The first pots pulled out of the ocean were overflowing, spilling out over the decks below. The crew, wearing heavy gloves, broke the lobster into two pieces, saving the tails. The tails are thrown down the hatch to the cleaning and packing room where I was in charge, gutting the tails with a stainless-steel pressurized straw and neatly packing them in cases of twenty-four, after which they were flash frozen. I listened to the Rolling Stones, Aerosmith, and Foreigner for hours, repeating the tedious steps for days.

Monotonous. I found myself daydreaming of European castles and designer clothes. And my beautiful fur coat.

At times, I took a break and walked up to the pilot house to see Terry. I had to walk through the engine room with its enormous machines, filters, water purifiers, and unbelievable noise. In the pilothouse was where all the navigation and fish finding equipment was housed. It looked like an airplane cockpit—sonar, radar, and all the communication devices to talk to the mainland or another boat in the area.

When Terry had to go down to the deck, he taught me how to pilot the boat, keeping this one-hundred-thirty-foot vessel moving forward at the right speed and staying close to the pots and their attached lines. One throttle was for speed and one throttle was the forward and reverse gears for the two engines. I learned how to maneuver the boat pretty well in rough seas. This lobster run was going to be profitable. Our tanks were full and we were heading back to port.

As the cook on this boat, we ate lobster almost every night. Damaged tails could not be sold so they brought them to the galley. I was frying, grilling, sauteing, battering, and boiling this succulent meat.

Dinner was the only time to rest when not sleeping. Somebody had to run the ship when the rest of the crew was eating or sleeping and it was always four-hour shifts. My shift was usually from eight to midnight.

We reached the Marianas for lobster fishing and needed two weeks to get back to Honolulu. On the return trip I felt a sharp pain in my lower abdomen and needed to see a doctor. I was in severe pain, worse than I'd ever felt before. We were so far away from the mainland and no doctors were in the middle of the Pacific. I found myself reflecting, realizing I was not meant to be a fisherman. This was not in my dreams and Terry was not going to be my Prince Charming.

Arriving in port, I was immediately driven to a hospital. I was diagnosed with an ectopic pregnancy, in surgery within an hour to remove the cyst that burst during the procedure. I'd come close to dying at sea. I called my mom to come rescue her daughter. Again.

Terry had to leave to go back out to sea, but I was done with my deep-sea adventures and with Terry. Mom stayed for a week, seeing me through recovery and helping me sort through my thoughts. Shannon and I were talking daily. Both of us were fed up with Seattle and the rain. We were both in our thirties, single, childless, and still dreaming of Cinderella. Our school was doing great, even though Seattle was in an economic decline. I was going to stay in Hawaii for a few months, then she and I would decide what we could do to change our lives.

When I could get up and walk, Mom took me shopping for a dress so I could search for a job, leaving my fishing days in the past. She never liked Terry — he was a very charming rogue, perhaps too much like my dad. Fun, entertaining, outgoing, but always getting into trouble. She knew I needed a pretty dress to snap back to my former self. I did my hair, donned a white linen dress with new white sandals, and walked into the Kahala Hilton — a luxury resort with white sandy beaches and swaying palm trees. Diamond Head was up ahead. There was a beautiful jewelry store off the entrance and I simply asked them did they needed any help? Yes, could you start tomorrow? Yes.

My first day on the job, Brigitte Nielson walked in. She was newly married to Sylvester Stallone, and shopping for bikinis and bling. The same week I saw Huey Lewis and Jerry Lewis. I quickly learned about jewelry, and met the star of Magnum P.I, Tom Selleck.

Hawaii was wonderful and a perfect recipe to reflect on one's inner being. I could calmly take account of what I had done and where I wanted to go in my next chapter of life.

My glamor was back and it was time to go see Shannon.

Chapter Four
California Girls

It was 1985, and Seattle was in the midst of the worst snowstorm ever. Shannon and I were definitely of the same mindset and knew we could do better than the Pacific Northwest. Neither of us wanted to live out our future in gray gloom, needing to get out of Seattle. Our school year was about over, so we could graduate the current students and simply not enroll anymore. We wanted out of the rain. How about California? Our experience together at the American Academy of Interior Design was wonderful. But we were gypsies at heart, wanting better weather where surely the grass would be greener and our options for men would be better. Flipping a coin, Beverly Hills beat out San Francisco.

We took several months to settle the school, pack up our furniture, all the while dreaming about sunshine. My old modeling agency booked me for a ten-day runway show at Nordstrom, paying me two thousand dollars. A lot of money. Shannon drove a BMW and I had an apartment full of furniture. We had no real plan, other than starting a new life.

Next steps: navigating a moving van, loading our belongings and telling the driver, "Deliver it to the Beverly Hills Hotel in three days."

We hopped in her car and headed south toward our new beginnings, never looking back.

Shannon had several job opportunities, and I was going to get my realtor's license. We road tripped from Seattle to Beverly Hills in about twenty hours, direct to the Beverly Hills Hotel. It was our dream destination, and a new future awaited us. We freshened our make-up in the car as we valet parked at the pink palace. It took us only one glass of champagne in the green velvet booths at the Polo Lounge to know we made the right decision. The wallpaper was covered in huge green palm fronds and I recognized famous faces strutting through the lobby. The pool had its pink and white covered cabanas where you could order chopped cobb salad and raspberry sorbet or simply more champagne. Famous names were paged on the public loudspeaker for telephone calls. Our eyes glistened with glee with so much going on.

Shannon's friend was living in a condo on Wilshire Boulevard, so we stayed the night there, hunting the next day for an apartment. We couldn't really deliver our furniture to the Beverly Hills Hotel.

We found a two bedroom on Beverly Glen Boulevard, not too far away from Westlake Village and Century City. Two days later our furniture arrived.

Shannon landed a job at Victoria's Secret on Pico Boulevard and I found a job at a new condo development in Century City. My first day on the job the owner, Ray Watt, introduced himself to me. After telling him a little about my story and my intent to get my realtor's license, he told me I could study all I want during my work hours and he knew I'd be a success. He was the owner and developer of so many high-rise buildings, I felt it was a good omen to work for him.

Studying for the real estate exam occupied my days, discovering Los Angeles filled my nights. We visited all the hot spots, cafes, boutiques, and restaurants from Beverly Hills to Malibu. Two new California girls on the scene. Our social calendar blossomed with dinners, dancing, parties, and of course lunch at the Polo Lounge. The company she worked for, Victoria's Secret, was really taking off and I was looking forward to my future in real estate representing celebrities.

In a few months I acquired my license. I interviewed at a few companies on Rodeo Drive. I chose a firm called Alverez, Hyland and Young on Canon Drive, next to the restaurant, Bistro Gardens. I was impressed with all of the owners, especially Elaine Young. Elaine offered to take me under her wing and introduce me to the Hollywood scene. She had been married to the actor, Gig Young, and knew everybody. She was blond, sexy, and lived in the world of Hollywood deals.

Elaine became my mentor, constantly complimenting me and boosting my confidence. I was so happy I left the dreariness of Seattle and was now surrounded by glamor everywhere I looked. In those days sex appeal sold Hollywood, and she was a firm believer in long blond hair and very short skirts. I fit the bill perfectly, having been a model for Versace only a few years prior. She loved that I had worked with Gianni in Milan, a life of fashion, playboys, and country estates. Here she would teach me the ropes in her world. I was going to be a real estate mogul!

I spent my days with Elaine, driving around town top down in her white Jaguar convertible, cruising the streets of Bel Air and Beverly Hills. Lunch at the Polo Lounge or the Bistro Gardens and evenings partying at the Playboy Club or Vertigo. These were the days of disco music, padded shoulders, car phones, and Michael Milken and his junk bonds. I was lucky to have met Elaine when I did. She firmly believed that a woman had to be cute enough to get in the door, then have the brains to back it up. My first sale to a B movie producer was a mansion in the Beverly Hills Flats for four-million dollars. My commission check was over twenty-five thousand dollars. I was in the right place at the right time.

I met Rod Stewart at Le Dome, danced with Prince, and dated Robert Davi, who was the star in the movie *Goonies*.

Together we sold a house to Don Cornelius of Soul Train and worked with Herb Alpert, Julie Andrews, and her dear friend Elaine Stritch. We attended parties hosted by Peter Nygaard, where he played the soundtrack of *Top Gun* continually at his Venice Beach house. I knew him before his feather parties of scantily clad wanna-be actresses became infamous. Everyone was doing drugs. I had visited that path in my twenties. I was not going to make it part of my lifestyle in my thirties and beyond. I had too much to do and needed to focus while enjoying the ride.

It was Thursday in Beverly Hills, meaning lunch at the Polo Lounge with Elaine. I found myself in the center of Hollywood selling luxury homes to the mega rich. She knew everyone, sitting next to Francesca Hilton and two of the Gabor sisters. The restaurant was always filled with Hollywood moguls, starlets, and aging screen stars. Joan Collins always made an entrance and George Hamilton had his own table.

Today she was going to play matchmaker, introducing me to someone, describing him as smart, sexy and handsome. I was in my mid-thirties and seriously looking for the man of my dreams to escape the life of the single girl. I was looking for cute enough to kiss, smart enough to talk to, wanting it all. I was wearing a canary yellow jacket and a very short black pencil skirt with killer black stilettos. I don't think I even owned flat shoes back then. Why?

Elaine introduced me to Larry Flax. We hit it off immediately. He was extremely, I mean over the top, handsome and had a great sense of humor. Tall, fit, and an amazing sense of style. He charmed us with stories of his new business venture, California Pizza Kitchen on South Beverly Drive. He was busy choosing logos and menus and commented on how striking my jacket was, such a bright intense yellow and he liked the contrast with the black. His menu was going to be unique pizza toppings like chicken and basil, smoked salmon and cream cheese, and BBQ chicken. He politely asked for my phone number and Elaine and I planning my future on the drive back to the office. Larry Flax.

We immediately started dating, frequenting all the hot-spots. Nicky Blairs, the Ivy, Bistro Gardens, and my favorite, Le Dome. He was social and fun, with a great group of friends, super smart and always smiling. The sexiest man alive, romantic and eager to please, we were naked a lot. I was always proud to be seen with him and I liked the chemistry between us. Dating Larry always meant trying new food combos that he could put on pizza. The dough was the platform and he didn't want to offer traditional fast-food recipes. This concept was going to be new and exciting and he was going to franchise his future stores and make millions. He had this fabulous home off of Coldwater Canyon, really close to where Elaine lived. The enormous bathroom was all glass and white marble with scented candles everywhere. His house was decorated in oversized white furniture with tons of pillows. True California casual chic. He had such good taste.

I was Elaine's roommate. Her home was a country French style rambler directly on Coldwater, overflowing with pink flowers. Begonias, hyacinths, lilies, and tulips covered her entrance and spilled out to her swimming pool. More potted pink flowers were throughout her garden, the fragrant smell, intoxicating. Her house was constantly filled with people, from her celebrity clients, to musicians, to the girls she wanted to help. There was always something to learn from Elaine. A master of connection.

Her daughter, Jennifer, was the love of her life. Elaine was a knockout in the sixties, a sex symbol who married the actor Gig Young. As his fourth wife, she got pregnant with his only child, Jennifer. Gig was known to be bisexual, and he contested paternity, so he and Jennifer never had a really great relationship. He committed suicide, a tragic ending. In those early days Elaine became a very successful Realtor, but she was always worried about her daughter.

Jennifer's best friend at the time was a brunette named Heidi Fleiss. Heidi was the Madam of a prostitution ring and owner of a famous black book containing every name and phone number in Hollywood and beyond. Heidi was living with her boyfriend, an international financier named Bernie Cornfield in an old broken-down mansion in Bel Air. He was friends with Hugh Hefner and Tony Curtis. It was a very decadent, opulent lifestyle. Elaine and I would zip up winding roads past heavily gated estates to Bernie's house when we couldn't locate Jennifer. Heidi's reputation was less than desirable, sporting dirty stringy hair and ripped clothes. It put Elaine in a constant state of worry.

Elaine was trying to help me make a living in real estate, so my days were busy. I was always at the office waiting for the phone to ring or for a client to walk in. I needed to sell a house or I couldn't pay rent. One morning the phone rang, and on the other end was a newbie to Los Angeles who left his job in Boston to work for the producer Steven Bochco on a new series called *LA Law*. His name, David E. Kelley. He needed a place to rent for a year until he got on his feet. I met him at the NBC Commissary when it was over on Olympic Boulevard in Century City. We shopped for houses to rent and he told me of his love for ice hockey. A couple years later, he was shopping for houses to buy, a two-million-dollar view property in the Hollywood Hills. He would go on to marry Michelle Pfeiffer. He was a true gentleman whose dream came true.

So, I was dating Larry and selling houses, and hanging out with Elaine. I was looking forward to perhaps a real relationship that would last longer than my usual three months. I looked at him as a true Prince Charming. Was he the one? Larry started taking yoga and met this girl named Joan. All of a sudden, he wanted to take more yoga classes and this Joan became the focus of his life. Dumped. The pizza ride was over. Couldn't keep crying over what was not meant to be. True love just wasn't in the picture for Larry and me. His logo became canary yellow and black. I would love to think I was his inspiration. It still makes me smile.

I earned enough money by 1989 to buy a condo on Wilshire Boulevard which I was able to flip and upgrade into a home just off Benedict Canyon on Davies Drive. It was one story, two bedrooms with a view of the canyons, only five minutes to Beverly Hills. I bought it from a developer I knew who also purchased the home of Roman Polanski on the street below mine, the scene of the infamous Charles Manson murders. It was now twenty years later and he was about to tear it down to build a mega mansion on the site. Would I like a tour before the demolition? Of course, I was curious.

Boarded up gates had no trespassing signs scrawled in huge letters. Driving up a winding driveway, we approached a single-story country style house with white paned windows and a dilapidated shingle roof. The French farm door was rusty and hard to open, cracking on its hinges. The house had rarely been entered since that fateful night. Still visible were writings on the wall painted in the blood of the victims. The furniture was intact from that capsule of time. We had read the newspaper clippings describing the fate of the beautiful pregnant Sharon Tate and Jay Sebring. We remembered photos of Charles Manson, Squeaky Fromm, and Tex Watson. This true Hollywood story was unforgettable. The bulldozers arrive to erase all memories of this horrific crime.

I need to get back to work and find a client. Recently, I purchased a Mercedes 380SLC with a car phone, and I now had a mortgage to pay. I'd been working a lot, living in Beverly Hills for the past five years. Shannon met a wonderful guy and was talking about getting married. I hoped marriage would be in the cards for me someday. But for now, I had to sit at my desk on Canon Drive and pray a client walked through the door.

Chapter Five

Romance at Last

Again, it was Thursday and I was looking forward to lunch at the Polo Lounge. Chopped salad and iced tea. Maybe we would sit at the pool? It was almost noon, and I applied a fresh coat of red lipstick. I could see the front door when a black Rolls-Royce pulled up. Three men emerged, making their way inside the office. They had an appointment and their agent was not around.

I winked at my co-worker. "This one's for me."

A unique trio. The one driving the Rolls Royce was dark-haired, fair-skinned, and wearing a black motorcycle jacket with shiny alligator shoes. I noticed he was acting as translator for the other two men, speaking both French and Portuguese. I recognized the one speaking French from my nights out with Elaine at Le Dome. He was the owner of the nightclub Vertigo and was dating the Princess of Monaco, Stephanie. The other one looked like an Elvis wanna-be, dressed head to toe in fringed white leather and oversized sunglasses. The trio made a strange first impression. I set my sights on selling a house.

I escorted the men upstairs to the glass conference room to talk business. The motorcycle jacket man, Ramon, did most of the talking.

They were looking for a house to buy for this Elvis look-a-like and his family. Turns out, he was a very wealthy Brazilian businessman, Jean Flavio, who owned oil wells and most of the cattle in Brazil. He desired a home in Trousdale with a pool and view. We poured over brochures and made appointments to tour these properties the next day. I was hoping to pay the mortgage on my Benedict Canyon house.

We talked for three hours about the market and what he needed in a home for his wife and kids. Ramon was translating and we were all laughing as the hours flew by. Ramon was Lebanese, speaking French, Arabic, English fluently and enough Portuguese to keep the conversation flowing, charming us with stories of Beirut, the Paris of the Middle East, and flirting with me. The afternoon slipped into early evening, and I missed lunch. All our appointments for tomorrow were set. Before leaving Ramon pulled me aside. Would I like to have dinner with him?

Now, I just met this guy, and he was definitely fun and entertaining. And there was a black Rolls-Royce outside. Hmmm, could be fun. Yes. I would meet him in two hours at his favorite Italian restaurant, Caffe Roma, just down the street on Canon Drive. I headed home to change and put on those black stilettos.

I wore red — I loved wearing red, always felt sexier and somehow a stronger woman — a Chinese red jacket with oversized shoulder pads made famous by Linda Evans in the TV show *Dynasty*. My skirt was a multi-colored chiffon, very short and full, flowing in the wind, and the black stilettos, the exclamation point. I parked my car behind Ramon's Rolls-Royce at the valet outside Caffe Roma, breezing into the restaurant. I was promptly escorted to his table. It was a lively place, white tablecloths, Italian music, and a big screen on the wall showing black and white movies. Sophia Loren, bigger than life gazing down on us. Champagne.

My first impression: successful, worldly, and utterly confident. He wore a diamond Rolex, a suit jacket, and those same alligator shoes I noticed earlier. His hands were soft, and he was well groomed, though I thought his hair was too long. He was attractive, dark and mysterious. A solid seven. Then he started telling stories, completely mesmerizing me with images of war-torn Beirut and the allure of the French Riviera.

I was familiar with pre-war Lebanon, during the days when Aristotle Onassis used to dock outside the Casino of Lebanon in his two-hundred-foot yacht overflowing with friends like Omar Shariff and Bridgette Bardot. It had been a time of royalty, oil rich sheikhs, and jetsetters between the cities of London, Athens, Paris, and Beirut. Movie stars mixing with Presidents, glamor ruling.

War broke out in Beirut in the early seventies spurring Ramon to leave for France to study International Politics. He studied at the Sorbonne in Paris and was hopeful about returning to Lebanon someday. He was raised Catholic, having a large family still living in Beirut, and he missed his two brothers deeply. He wanted to fulfill his American dream of marrying the tall blond girl driving the red Ferrari and drinking Coca-Cola. I guess we all loved Christy Brinkley. We made an unusual but comfortable fit. He told me he wanted children, and his rating shot up to ten.

Ramon was an entrepreneur down to his core and was always on the hunt for ways to bend the rules of finance to make a fortune. Over dinner, I was intrigued by the ways of the Middle East, and in awe of his views on making money. The way he spoke about business, making millions, effortlessly. Buying cheap, selling high, and buying millions at a time so the commission is always a fortune.

As dizzying as his business acumen was, equally was his cultural depth. He spoke four languages.

He was knowledgeable about the great cities of the world, and where to go and what to eat in each one. He painted a lush picture of a lifestyle filled with exotic travel, friends and family. He dreamed of political aspirations when the current situation in Lebanon settled. Right there and then, at our first dinner, I imagined spending the rest of my life with him. Was this love at first sight?

Dinner was ending, and a simple brown paper bag was placed on the table between us.

"Open it, it's a small token for you."

Inside the bag was a Bulgari diamond and gold watch. I thought I hit the jackpot and all my dreams were coming true. Was Ramon my Prince Charming? Was I his Cinderella? He asked me to lunch the next day. I already knew what I was going to wear.

I'd never dated someone who showered me with gifts like Ramon did. Every day the Rolls-Royce stopped by to deliver bouquets of flowers, boxes of candy, cases of champagne, and exotic foods in opulent gift baskets. We dined at all the best restaurants in Beverly

Hills: Spago, Il Pastaio, L'Orangerie. Making me feel like I was one in a million and I was made for him. I saw him as an exotic adventurer from a foreign land, mysterious, intelligent and needing a partner in life. He swept me off my feet and now there was no looking back.

He bought me jewelry laden with sapphires, diamonds, rubies, emeralds, and gold. It was an otherworldly courtship. No one had given me such treasures. I was in awe of his limitless generosity. I felt so special when I was with him, wondering if he was like that with every woman he met. He must be very successful, I thought, to afford this splendor, and I knew my life with him would be very different from my simpler beginnings. We were spending all our days together and I had no time for real estate. After a week together, we were inseparable.

He was living in a one-story bachelor pad in Trousdale right next to Danny Thomas with a killer view and a huge swimming pool. It was decorated in black leather, shiny black marble tables, and sleek travertine floors. Signed photographs of naked models lined the walls and an enormous television filled the living area. It was never quiet, as he loved an entourage. He had maids, drivers, attorneys, and deal makers constantly walking through the doors. When we ordered lunch or dinner, it was enough to feed an army. There were a lot of Lebanese men coming in and out speaking Arabic, and I didn't understand a word. Arabic was spoken constantly, and I tried to pick up a few words, thinking it was so exotic and he was so fascinating.

His business, he explained, was buying and selling cosmetics. He traveled to Las Vegas and New York frequently, and I immediately started going with him. Always first class and always staying in the best hotels. In New York, we visited the offices of Liz Claiborne, Paco Rabanne, and Revlon. I witnessed Ramon in action, charming the sales force to sell him millions of dollars of product for use in the casinos. Las Vegas was booming, the Mirage had just been built, and their CEO Steve Wynn was on a roll. Michael Millken's junk bonds were fueling casino expansion on the Vegas strip. Ramon introduced me to Steve and Elaine Wynn, then Terri Lanni, the CEO of Caesars World. They were spending billions on the new Las Vegas and Ramon wanted to be a part of it, supplying the thousands of new rooms with his amenities and VIP gifts. Every new casino had over three thousand rooms and Ramon was supplying shampoo and soap in every room, every day. Business is a numbers game, and Vegas was his town.

He was a gambler at heart both on and off the casino floor, acting like money grew on trees.

I sat at the tables, watching him win or lose thousands of dollars. This was big money to me. I had stars in my eyes, staying at the best suites in the casinos, dining in the top restaurants, and visiting the spas. Driving up to the valet in his black Phantom Rolls Royce. "Mr. D., welcome back, so nice to see you again!" Tipping hundred-dollar bills to everyone. Signing restaurant checks with a flourish. There were always perks on the house.

My boyfriend was considered a VIP Whale, a term given to the big gamblers in Las Vegas. The casinos spoil their customers with anything they want just so they stay at the tables and hopefully lose. And they lost big, very big—losing fortunes and thinking the next spin of the roulette wheel would give them back what they lost. An unyielding hope. When Ramon won, it was a fairytale. When he lost, well, that was another story.

When he won, he would take me shopping anywhere I wanted. Cartier, Dior, and Chanel. He loved buying me fabulous clothes and spoiling me in the shops of the big casinos. Sometimes we'd go across the street to Neiman Marcus and have personal shoppers set me up in a private room and bring fabulous items for me to try. The personal shoppers knew my affinity for Fendi and Versace.

When he lost, he was a man I didn't know. Dark, moody, angry at the world. Screaming at his associates and glaring at me like I jinxed him. I had to keep quiet until his mood passed, fearful of him lashing out at me. I hoped these moments would fade and somehow our relationship would evolve into one of constant kindness and respect. I felt he needed me to calm him and reassure him all would be okay. It was just a glimpse into a complicated mind and I hoped I had the patience to ride it out. I was now thirty-seven and ready to make this relationship work. He really wanted to take care of me and I wanted love.

He asked me to marry him three months after we met, presenting me with a six-carat white diamond, the exact one Mickey Rooney gave to Ava Gardner. Emerald cut. I said yes in a heartbeat. By marrying Ramon, I could finally escape my past and live a glamorous life filled with kids and prosperity. I'd known I would find true happiness one day, and in Ramon I finally found my soulmate, my Prince Charming from all those fairytales. I was going to live like a queen!

Chapter Six

Ramon

Ramon Antoine Abi-Rached was born in Beirut in 1950. In those days, the jetsetters of the world would divide their time between Monte Carlo, Athens, and Beirut, sometimes stopping in London, Paris, or New York. Beirut was called the Paris of the Middle East, rich with elegant shops, sidewalk bistros, and all-night parties. The Casino du Liban sat high on the hill overlooking the Bay of Jounieh, filled with the yachts of Aristotle Onassis, the Aga Khan, and oil rich Sheikhs of Saudi Arabia.

Lebanon declared its independence from France in 1943, but still maintained close ties.

Everyone spoke Arabic and French, welcoming Charles De Gaulle as a war hero. Life in the Middle East after World War II was complicated, to say the least. The Jewish state was created, setting the stage for a return to their promised land, creating a situation whereby the displaced Palestinians had to leave their country with no specific place to go, relocating to Egypt, Syria, and Lebanon without money, jobs, or citizenship.

Lebanon welcomed the refugees but did not give them legal citizenship. The Palestinians were a people without a country. The

Jewish state initially had good relations with their neighbors. In the democratic politics of Lebanon, a balance of power between religions was always carefully apportioned between Sunni, Shiite, Druze, Catholic, and Orthodox. The idea of bestowing citizenship upon a mostly Sunni population would upset the balance.

Ramon lived a very European lifestyle in pre-civil war Beirut. Days filled with shopping at French boutiques and jewelry stores. Drinking an espresso at a small café in the afternoon, or perhaps a lunch onboard someone's yacht. Evenings were spent at the grand Casino Du Liban. The Middle East was still developing, and newly rich oil Sheikhs would crowd into Beirut, enjoying the nights filled with belly dancers, hookah pipes, and oriental pleasures. It was a country of opposites, a true mix of cultures from the east and west.

Men bragging about being Phoenicians, the old-world traders of the Orient. They considered themselves cleverer than any foreigner, always able to turn sand into gold. They were from the land of the fertile Bekaa Valley where Roman armies roamed. It was the center of the Crusades battles, now filled with Roman temples and amphitheaters strewn everywhere from Baalbek to Byblos to Beirut. All remnants of a great city at the hub of ancient civilization. Wars were fought over three centuries between Muslims, Christians, and Jews and still the battle had not been won.

Ramon was from a sect called Maronite Catholic, named after Syrian born St. Maron. This sect flourished in the region close to the famous Cedars of Lebanon, not far from the village of Ramon's ancestors, Bejdarfel, in the county of Batroun, situated between the seashore port of Byblos and the valley of Baalbek. Ramon's grandfather's brother was a priest who built a home with a small chapel. The clan Abi-Rached, now numbering close to one hundred, still frequents this family-owned chapel.

Catholic traditions run deep in the Abi-Rached clan. Ramon and his brothers attended a private boarding school run by Jesuit priests, and his sisters attended the religious schools run by Catholic nuns. He was the youngest of five children, spending most of his youth away at boarding school, alone, his older siblings leaving for marriage or universities. He missed out on the closeness of family life, looking up to his brothers.

In 1967 Israel invaded Lebanon and intense fighting broke out. Thousands of Palestinian militants (PLO) under Yassar Arafat were pouring into the country, escaping the war in Palestine. Complicating matters, Lebanese civil war broke out between the Muslims and the Christians in 1975. Ramon left the country in these tumultuous times and went to France for studies. It was the right time to get out.

He studied political science and international politics at universities in Toulouse and Paris. His father was a medical doctor, and begged Ramon to follow. After fainting at the sight of blood in the first year of medical school, he changed his course of study to politics. The Lebanese constitution is divided to give a triumvirate of power whereby the President must be Christian, the Prime Minister be Sunni Muslim, and the Speaker of the House be Shiite Muslim. Ramon's birthright gave him the right to someday be elected President and he was going to study with that in mind.

Ramon was a serious student, completing his thesis in international politics and taking a position as an attaché with UNESCO, hoping to return to Lebanon. With war still raging, his hopes of working in his own country with the United Nations were crushed. Remaining with UNESCO was tearing him apart. So, what does a creative Phoenician do? He started selling fancy soaps door to door in France! He would tote around luxury soap in his fancy red sports car, charming all his neighbors, until he had enough money for a plane ticket to America.

A lot of Lebanese fled during the civil war and went to Cleveland, Detroit, or Los Angeles. Ramon left France for Detroit where he had an Uncle Woody. It was a brief interlude before the excitement of Las Vegas beckoned. There were junkets in the seventies full of wannabe gamblers on chartered flights departing the major cities direct to Las Vegas. Ramon stepped off the plane into his newfound paradise. He was hooked. Bright lights, girls, gambling, and more gambling. He hit the casinos with a passion.

On one of these junkets, he met a Lebanese woman by the name of Dolores Owens. She was a Vice President at Caesars Palace in charge of high-roller clients. It was prior to the Mirage or Bellagio casinos being built and Caesars was the major player at the time. Dolores was developing her clientele of Middle Eastern and Asian gamblers and needed some expensive gifts to give away. Could Ramon find something different? Of course, he was a Phoenician, a trader by birth.

He spoke French, knew about perfume and soap, so he started importing big brands like Baccarat, Lalique, Saint Louis, and

Guerlain. Fred Hayman had just released a fragrance called 273, and YSL's Opium was the hottest thing on the market. He started buying large quantities and opened a shop on Spring Mountain Road called Partout. In French, it means everywhere. Soon all the casinos were buying from him. His personal clients were Liberace, Elvis, Phyllis MacGuire, and a few mobsters who wandered in looking for gifts for their girlfriends.

Business was booming, and his cars got fancier. He wanted to grow, to build a huge business. He discovered he could entice the manufacturers to sell to the booming casino market as promotional advertising (mainly golf tournaments) and they would cut their prices. And here's the twist. If he could buy enough quantities, he'd resell these luxury brands to the big retail stores with a lot more profit than by selling small quantities to the casinos. There were only a few golf tournaments requiring these gifts for giveaways, but a huge market by reselling to major retail outlets.

By buying and reselling high-end merchandise, Ramon was entering into what's called the gray market of diverting goods. At the time, it was perfectly legal, as he owned the merchandise. Some of the prestigious manufactures with fancy French names didn't want to sell directly to discount stores like Phar-Mor, so they sold to a Lebanese businessman called Ramon Abi-Rached. Ramon felt he would create a better marketing profile, not as a Middle Eastern, but as a Frenchman, by reinventing himself. So, when he became a US citizen, he simply raised his right hand, gave his pledge allegiance to our flag and translated his name from Ramon Abi-Rached to Ramon DeSage. This is the man that would charm and woo me and I would agree to marry. Monsieur Ramon Antoine DeSage.

Ramon could now invite his manufacturers to Las Vegas to show them where he would be placing their product. He had a Rolls-Royce and a penthouse suite in one of the top casinos. Ramon would stock the suite with his soaps and perfumes and luxury gifts, showing them how their product would be showcased. The hook was set, would they take the bait? Front row seats to shows, money to gamble, first class dining. The best Las Vegas had to offer. They only needed to sell Ramon the goods, and they could hardly wait to sign.

Ramon discovered in those early days that he made making money seem easy. Other people wanted in. He could actually get investors to fund his purchase orders prior to a signed contract. He could get millions of dollars of product on a signature and resell it without even taking delivery. This was the gray market as a middleman to real shops, real customers, real buyers, and eager customers. It was the beginning of using other people's money. He could now buy the goods on a proforma invoice, shop the buyer, secure the down payment, and roll over the goods. He kept commissions on the deals and the deals were huge.

Over time, it just got too tempting. The size of the orders continued to grow bigger, meaning enormous amounts of money exchanging hands. Some of it was bound to get lost on the tables. The lure of double or nothing by a simple spin of the roulette. Big money loses its value and becomes a game of risk. The real world stops when the sun goes down. The bright lights of Las Vegas beckon and call the players to the table. Roll the dice a few times and maybe hit it big. It was a roller coaster of adrenaline.

To get away from it all, California was right next door. Caesars corporate office was in Beverly Hills and he had few friends there. New clients could be found, new investors just waiting to be tapped.

Ramon rented a house in Trousdale and furnished it with all the latest electronics and gadgets a high-roller bachelor needed. Nights were spent at the Playboy club and the trendy restaurants on Sunset Boulevard. He was now forty years of age, dating models and dancers and trying to keep the money tree filled. His friend Jean Flavio called and wanted to buy a house; did Ramon know any real estate agents? They hopped in the Rolls, grabbed Mario, and headed down Hillcrest towards Canon Drive to the office of Elaine Young, where they were greeted by a tall buxom blond in a fiery red jacket, named Debra.

Chapter Seven

The Dark Side of Glamor

I discovered he had a very dark, moody downside when he lost at the tables. He became so angry and terrified of anyone approaching him when the cards weren't going his way. We were all bad luck and somehow jinxing him. The Bellagio had recently opened and we were staying in one of their VIP suites. I retired early to our suite; bored, fearful he was losing. I left him sitting at the table, knowing this night was different. He was down over one hundred thousand dollars.

Opening the door around midnight, he screamed at me, "You fucking whore, you're making my life miserable!"

The verbal became physical. He pushed me to the ground. Instincts had me trying to get to the door to escape, but he kicked me in the stomach with those alligator shoes. Reasoning with him, telling him I loved him, I was terrified. He turned around and picked up a chair, throwing it at me and breaking it into pieces, barely missing me. The sound of the chair seemed to shock him, and he apologized, but I had bruises on my arm and my stomach, and the chair was evidence of his wrath.

I'd never been with a man who was violent, and of course, he apologized and took me on a major shopping spree. I assured myself he would control his anger and with my help he would lighten up on the gambling. What were my options? I was now thirty-seven years old, wanting kids, and I truly thought with patience and a little time, we could work this out. It had only been a little domestic incident, after all. I let it go.

In the in-between, he constantly charmed me with stories of pre-war Lebanon. The yachts, the jewels, and the jet-set life mixing Middle Eastern cultures with French diplomats. It was an international lifestyle of Saudi Arabian businessmen having mountains of money and spending it in the souks of Beirut. There were tales of war and fleeing your home country, of militia occupying every corner of the city and every museum being ransacked, of banks being broken into and all the riches stolen. Tales of the ancient Phoenicians on their routes between Venice and Egypt. He was so much fun, entertaining his entourage for hours.

Personally, I have always dreamed of Hollywood, Paris, and New York. I'd have loved to have been a movie star with all the lights on me. I was seduced by it all: the costumes, lighting, makeup, sets, scenery, and fairytale stories. Mom and I used to sit for hours watching AMC and TCM classic old movies, memorizing the lines of Rita Hayworth, Stewart Granger, Clark Gable, Cary Grant, Gene Kelly, and Cyd Charisse. I'm sure we watched, *Singing in the Rain* twenty times. With my small-town roots, I never lost hope of finding my Prince Charming.

Innocent and gullible, I fell for Ramon's hustle, hook, line and sinker. I'd never met a true seducer, a man with charm and a Rolls-Royce. I was the blond bombshell without the hardened exterior, an easy mark, and I wanted to believe he was special. I was overtaken by his world of jewels, jets, recognition sitting at his table, hypnotized by his charisma. We all were. It was a life of travel, easy money, and rubbing elbows with the rich and famous.

Quite possibly I'd been seduced by the smoothest con artist of all time—I was not alone. He had a special gift of conviction, the ability to draw people into his web. We were all content to be in his world, a life looking through rose-colored glasses. I had a front row seat, watching him wheel and deal with clients in New York, Paris, and Las Vegas, convinced he was on his way to great success. I ignored his Middle Eastern attitudes of complete control and lack of respect for women, looked the other way when it came to his out-of-control gambling habits. My clock was ticking. I wanted to get married, knowing I'd have a very colorful life with Ramon, perhaps finding love. I was going to overlook the anger, the gambling, and his questionable business tactics for a fairytale life. I knowingly gambled with my heart and dreams. A high-risk game. Who's gambling now?

It was 1990. Our first year together revolved around our stays at the Bellagio in Las Vegas or the Helmsley Palace in New York. We were spending so much time in New York where all the major cosmetic and fragrance companies had their headquarters. We lived in a suite on the fiftieth floor of the Helmsley when Leona and Harry Helmsley were living there. They owned quite a few of the major hotels in New York at the time. He was about ninety years old and she had the reputation of being a true screaming bitch, wheeling him in his wheelchair every night to a table next to ours in the dining room, feeding him chicken soup. There was a constant flow of visitors to the table through dinner and her voice was always angry and shouting. Not one of the employees in the hotel had a kind word to say about her. She was in the midst of an investigation for tax evasion. Why should the rich pay taxes? Harry soon died and she went to jail.

We stayed six months at the Helmsley Palace, then rented an apartment on 57th and Park Avenue in the Galleria. Fabulous views of the city and nearby Central Park, right next to Chanel and we would walk everywhere. Our apartment was on the forty-first floor and Eric Clapton was just above on the fiftieth floor. We were there the day his little boy tragically fell out the window.

There were daily meetings with all the perfume manufacturers and the gray market buyers. Each office was more opulent than the next, usually located on the top floor of a tall intimidating high rise. I went to appointments at Revlon, L'Oréal, and Liz Claiborne with top executives who would have the authority to sign off on a major discounted sale. Ramon wanted me on his arm when entering the offices, making a statement as a very sophisticated power couple. It was here I learned a new term: diversion.

Ramon was buying goods from the manufacturers with the stated intent to place them in the casino market. Instead, he sold to another distributor who in turn would resell to Walmart and Phar-Mor. Prospects were unlimited and the transactions extremely profitable. He refused to involve me in his business, always so vague. I started to question how he made his money, out of curiosity at first. He was purchasing truckloads of product, but we didn't have employees, a truck, or a warehouse. So where did the goods go?

He included me in most of the meetings with clients. Perhaps I softened the narrative and allowed Ramon to subtly convince his target we were just a nice couple from Las Vegas trying to build a business within the casino industry. Perhaps the clients appreciated when the conversation was getting too intense and I could ask about their wife or family. Maybe Ramon needed a wing man. Somehow it was working. Ramon walked out of the meetings with a signed proforma, or an intent to sell from the manufacturers. Then he started making calls to finance the deal with other people's money, and in a few short hours the deal was done. After a hectic day of business, we usually had dinner listening to Bobby Short playing the piano at the Cafe Carlyle. Then back to Las Vegas. Whirlwind.

It was June of 1991. We had a fight over something small and I stormed out the door, ending up on my mom's doorstep, crying for two days. This Frog Prince was turning out to be a toad after all. A few days later, he was banging on my mom's front door, apologizing of course, and pleading with me not to leave. Is this the only scenario where a man finally realizes it's time to tie the knot or lose the girl?

An ultimatum was given, love me or leave me. He was sweating, calling his lawyer. The next day we drove to the Little White Wedding Chapel, paying five hundred dollars for a wedding package, which included two photos and a VHS cassette. The prenup was in tow and I had my dress, our chauffeur was the witness. We drank champagne and Caesars Palace gave us a cake. This was my wedding day, without family or friends. Married.

Mom was thrilled and my sisters were happy for me. Everyone loved Ramon. The phone lines were open to Beirut, so we called his family with the news of our wedding. His two brothers begged us to visit right away, so perhaps a honeymoon in Beirut was the perfect plan. Of course, we stopped in Paris and visited the French Riviera on our way to meet the family. Our courtship had taken us several times through France, and I'd been listening to cassettes on how to speak French. I could now say bonjour and order my croissants et café au lait. That was about it.

We were living life at warp speed, taking the Concorde on a three-hour flight from New York to Paris, sitting next to Paul and Linda McCartney. When in Paris, we stayed at the Hotel de Crillon near the Louvre Museum. Monsieur Tonseth, the director of the hotel, gave us the corner suite overlooking the Place de la Concorde. It was decorated in navy blue velvet with a private sitting room and enormous balcony. I loved having breakfast in their yellow marble dining room with the huge chandeliers, then walking up the Champs-Élysées towards the Arc du Triomphe. We ate pâté de foie gras at the Moulin Rouge, drank magnums of pink champagne, and went shopping at Chanel. It was wildly romantic, and we talked about how happy we were. I was a galaxy away from Seattle, in so many ways.

Renting a car, we drove for two weeks through the French countryside, staying at different chateau's every night. We imagined buying one for our new home and even found a property surrounded by a moat filled with swans. We arrived in Monaco to celebrate its seven-hundred-year anniversary. Ramon tipped one thousand dollars to get us the best table at L'Hermitage Hotel, where they had a menu accentuated by black truffles. Wearing a thirty-carat emerald, I raised my glass of Dom Perignon, secretly saying prayers my bubble wouldn't burst.

We ended up in Cannes, staying at the Carlton on the beach. The hotel's beach was decorated with blue and white umbrellas strewn on the sand, and they served fresh juices called tutti frutti in frosted glasses while we rested in our lounge chairs. I bought a huge white hat and wore a white bathing suit, feeling like Rita Hayworth. Gazing out from under the brim, scanning the Bay of Cannes, I thought I married well.

After a week of lobster bouillabaisse, speedboats to the Isle St. Marguerite, and a few visits to the Casino in Monte Carlo, we were ready to depart for Beirut. I had a suitcase of new clothes from Paris.

I was ready to meet the family. Knowing Beirut would be fabulous, visions of sugar plums danced in my head.

The Beirut International Airport had recently reopened. On approach, I could see the white beaches, blue water, and a city of skyscrapers below. A new world of adventure lay beneath our wings.

Chapter Eight

Machine Guns and Little Lambs

Landing on the bumpy runway, full of pot holes, I got my first glimpse into a third world, post-war country, prior to reconstruction. It was unsettling. There were soldiers everywhere, machine guns draped as casually as my Chanel crossbody bag. I was afraid these guns would fire randomly and blow my head off. Army jeeps screeched by, everyone yelling in Arabic. We walked across the tarmac, no terminal, and the authorities took my passport. Surely now I'd be kidnapped and beheaded. Should I cover my hair? Was my skirt too short? Would I be arrested for grabbing Ramon's arm? I was petrified.

Women seemed to be covered, or at least more than I. I didn't know the difference between the laws in Saudi Arabia and the other countries in the Middle East. Ramon kept telling me not to worry. Lebanon was mostly Christian and very European in their culture. We were greeted by his family and everyone was crying, having been so long since seeing their brother, and now a new wife. All of us embraced in the midst of the chaos. Getting our passports back from the militia, I breathed a sigh of relief, and we drove in a caravan of cars toward their homes in the north.

Army checkpoints were everywhere. Our passports were stamped at customs and every soldier with a machine gun asked to see our papers. Driving through the war-torn city, we saw bombed out buildings so neglected that huge trees were growing out of their cement shells, branches popping out of third floor windows, no glass windows or front doors to be seen. Major streets once lined with glamorous shops were now home to wild dogs and flocks of pigeons.

We traveled further north to a city called Jounieh, where the infamous Casino du Liban was situated on the top of the corniche. It was such a beautiful bay, but long gone were the sleek yachts and elegant restaurants from the golden days of the sixties. There was nothing to remind you this was a paradise destination for the jetsetters of the past. It was a wreck, dirt everywhere, mountains of garbage lining the streets.

We arrived at a tiny hotel; three stars printed on the banner outside. Having left the Carlton Hotel in Cannes just a few hours earlier, I was somehow expecting something similar. This hotel was worse than an old boyfriend's dormitory on spring break. I watched the bell boys carry my Louis Vuitton suitcases up the stairs while we checked in. I guess I should have packed lighter. At least we were here in the country Ramon had spoken of every day for the last year. I would embrace his family and each day with an open mind to discover what it was he thought was so special. At the moment I still had my passport, and I was not being featured on CNN as a hostage situation in progress.

The family was so happy Ramon and I had traveled so far for this visit. The war was barely over and neither tourists nor extended family members were returning to this ravaged and dilapidated country. They made every effort to welcome me into the family, though our language barrier made communicating difficult. Mostly Arabic was spoken and a lot of French, a little English for my benefit. I made a mental note to buy a Berlitz book on speaking French before returning.

My first impressions: dirty streets and smoke-filled cafes. The sidewalk cafes displayed these oversized water pipes called nargile, or hookah pipes, filled with strong tobacco sitting on every table in every restaurant. My eyes focused on the bombed-out buildings, the dead dogs and cats on the streets. There were no stop signs, no white lines, and no rules of the road while driving. Whoever got there first had the right of way. At every turn there was another checkpoint, someone to take away my passport.

We drove along the coast, heading farther north and turning toward the mountains, and arriving at his ancestral village, Bejdarfel. Ramon glowingly spoke of it so many times, I was expecting the Garden of Eden, not this small rural community of less than three thousand inhabitants. It dated back to the days when the Egyptians would cut down the Lebanese Cedars, then transport these giant trees by elephants to the Mediterranean Sea. This little village had been on the elephant walk between the Pharaohs of Egypt and the Phoenicians. I was transported back in time to traveling by camel while dressed in silken capes and meeting the other Queens of the desert. Magical.

It was a simple village with a view of the mountains, next to the sea and totally undeveloped. Olive trees, grape vines, and fresh tomatoes filled all the small gardens. The smell of the lemon trees hung in the air. The homes were built with hand-carved stone blocks, surrounding the large chapel with a huge steeple and enormous church bell. Everything was so calm. The whole village greeted us, bringing a lamb hoisted high on their shoulders, laying it at our feet, cheering, and then slitting its throat. I knew it was an honor, but the blood from this sacrificial lamb was running near my new pale green Escada shoes. I was surely out of my element.

Ramon and I were lifted on their shoulders, and they carried both of us to the village center where we were the guests of honor at their traditional celebration feast: tabouli, fried potatoes, chicken shish taouk, and lots of arak, the local drink. We ate the lamb, so it didn't die in vain. It was so full of life, smiles, and simple affection. Everyone spoke Arabic, and I thought to myself how could I remember all these strange names so difficult to pronounce. Khairellah, Sleiman, Majid, it seemed so ancient. I felt like I was Lawrence of Arabia in the midst of the desert.

They kept yelling "Sheik!" at Ramon and calling me "Sheika!" I would learn later this was a title of honor having been passed down through generations from one feudal leader to the next. I was a girl from Seattle being called a "Sheika" and carried through the streets, watching them wave their machine guns in celebration. Tradition. Beautiful. Belonging.

We toured the village, meeting all the elders, the priests, and the entire Abi-Rached clan. Ramon changed his name to DeSage in America, but we were all Abi-Rached here. There was still a property with Ramon's old summer home on it, a tiny house given to one of Ramon's brothers. Next to it stood the family chapel, St. Antoine de Padua, large enough to seat fifty people, Maronite Catholic with a huge bell tower and built from enormous hand carved stones. The chapel was situated next to a private cemetery, where tradition allowed the men of the clan to be buried. Unmarried women were permitted burial here only to carry on the family name. It was the Middle East, after all, and I had so many traditions to learn. The chapel had an overwhelming charm. Its view of the mountains was magnificent, and I sensed a feeling of family and heritage.

Ramon suggested building a home here where he was emotionally connected to the land of his father, a pied-a-terre where we could visit his family and live between two worlds. I was thrilled with the idea; it would be an adventure. We'd had a home in Las Vegas in the center of Sin City, and Lebanon was a new world I was ready to embrace. We could build a home filled with traditions in which to raise our future family. It was such an easy decision. Ramon let me build whatever I wanted, opening our doors to this ancient world. We would create our own little chateau like those we visited on the outskirts of Paris. I imagined a real home complete with a chapel, surrounded by olive trees, living life happily ever after.

The next few weeks were spent buying land in the village surrounding our dream home and making connections for possible business ventures in post war Lebanon. Politicians circled Ramon and business opportunities were presented at every possible occasion. Lunches and dinners turning into meetings to create a new modern country with every technology imaginable. Energy deals, cell phone deals and even a chance to enter politics were on the table. Ramon seemed to be re-energized with all the potential avenues of deal-making. I thought we had a chance to become the power couple he thought we were.

Would this new world be my destiny?

It was the Paris of the Middle East after all, but it wasn't Paris. We hired an architect and started making plans for a grand chateau we would fill with children. The family was grateful and shed tears welcoming their brother back home. Ramon and I were ebullient, deciding to make Lebanon our home for generations to come. We only stayed a week, but left the country with dreams of building a castle in the sky in a country on the brink of post-war reconstruction. We were determined to be a big part of this new vision.

I had no idea I was agreeing to build a prison for myself, surrounded not by fruit trees, but by Mafia-type figures watching my every move. It was so easy to open the door to this new pathway, and it would take a lifetime to run for the exit.

Chapter Nine

Gamblin' Man

Ramon was a very difficult person to live with, gambling every night, literally every single night. We would drive to the casino, joke with the VIP valet, handing him a hundred-dollar bill for the privilege of parking one of our Rolls Royce at the prestigious entrance.

"Mr. D., so nice to see you," chimed the valet, confirming Ramon's status as a bigshot VIP. Then we would enter the casino and proceed to the gaming area.

It was either blackjack or video poker high stakes, three hundred dollars per pull on the slot machine. He only wanted to hit a jackpot, nothing else mattered. Arriving at the tables, the host would approach Ramon, handing him what looked like a blank check they would fill out together in the form of an IOU. It was a casino marker. Depending on his line of credit for the evening, the amount ranged from ten thousand, to twenty thousand dollars or more. Some whales sign markers for millions.

One of the employees in his entourage would always meet us on the casino floor, remaining several feet behind us while my husband played. I never noticed Ramon was constantly sliding casino chips to this gofer to go cash in at the Cashiers Cage. Ramon was signing the markers, but always leaving with bags of cash, perhaps ten thousand, sometimes a hundred thousand dollars, later making a deal with the casino before paying back these markers. They would always settle for a discount.

Ramon was gambling like a millionaire with money to burn, always doubling up, playing several hands at once. When he was winning, I stayed with him at the tables. I was lucky. When he was losing, he would look at me like I was the devil, call me a "fucking bitch," then hand me a thousand dollars to walk away from the table. I would spend the rest of the evening shopping—that's why I loved the Wynn Hotel. I usually went straight to Chanel, putting a deposit on a cute little alligator handbag, knowing tomorrow I would be back with the rest of the cash. We were there after all, every night, and he always paid me not to jinx him.

When on a losing streak, he sent me home with one of his employees. When winning, he's show up with a bag of cash. If he won, no problems. If he lost, he blamed me for his bad luck. I found it easier to not get involved and stay away from him during his gambling hours. We rarely had friends with us as Ramon liked to gamble alone. The casino host happily kept me company, wanting to keep his top whale at the table. The host, always charming and great fun, escorted me to all the shows, sometimes taking me shopping. I probably saw each Cirque du Soleil a dozen times.

If we went to dinner, it was to entertain his prospective clients who were trying to sell Ramon goods. Ordering expensive bottles of red wine: Petrus, Opus One, and Mouton Cadet de Rothschild. I loved the cascading piles of seafood and decadent desserts. I was arm candy, wearing my lavish jewels, sharing with our guests about our trips to the south of France and Lebanon. Five-hundred-dollar tips always went to the waiter and another five hundred to meet the chef. Then with a flourish, he'd sign the check, which was always, "Complimentary of the house, Mr. D."

Ramon was a VIP whale in the casino system, and everything was offered to keep him at the tables. He kept a penthouse suite upstairs for his clients. We had the use of the spas, along with all their treatments, and frequently reserved one of those private cabanas at the pool. We could book any restaurant, reserve any front row seat for whatever show was playing. Personally, I liked *Phantom of the Opera* and Andrea Boccelli. My husband never accompanied me—he was at the tables, losing money, keeping his VIP treatment. His focus was singular.

His gambling was an addiction and I didn't know how to deal with it. Ramon never admitted to having a problem. It reached a point early on in our marriage whereby I wasn't allowed to question his actions or thoughts. His word was law. He studied at a university and I studied at a modeling school. My arguments were without merit. The gambling would lead to extreme moments of euphoria, and then to a deep, dark anger. Sometimes I was unable to recognize the person in front of me.

He lashed out at me whether losing money on the tables or when a business deal soured. The anger lasted an hour or days, and I dealt with it by never opening a topic that could enrage him, sticking to fashion, family, or weather — never politics, religion, or money. Disagreeing secretly in my own thoughts, I learned to never challenge him. I married a narcissist, outspoken and arrogant, where no one's opinions mattered but his own. After an outburst, there was usually peace for a few days whereby I could breathe easier. I justified the perks of the casinos to escape from the dark atmosphere of my marriage. His gambling was providing my refuge.

We traveled back and forth between Las Vegas and visiting his family in Lebanon. We were serious about building a second home on our ancestral plot. Ramon could work at his business in Vegas and continue with his love of gambling, and I could focus on building a home and filling it with children overseas, embracing the chance of living between these two polar opposite worlds. Perhaps, I could entice Ramon to spend more time in his beloved Lebanon. Perhaps, a new life outside the casinos would enable Ramon to appreciate his marriage. I loved him when he was away from the tables with his feet on the ground, dreaming of new deals.

Las Vegas never seemed to be a place in which to raise kids; it was Sin City, filled with easy money, prostitutes, fancy cars, built on gambling, which I hate. Ramon, however, relished the bright lights and the songs of the slot machines on the casino floor. In Lebanon, I would raise our family in a village away from shopping malls and teenage drug use. It sounded perfect, and I convinced myself this was my way to getting Ramon out of Las Vegas. It was a long shot I was willing to take.

I never made significant friends in Las Vegas. The constant gambling never gave us the opportunity to entertain anyone except clients.

We were invited frequently to dine with Steve Wynn at his casino. Terri Lanni, at MGM, and Sir Robert Earl, President of Planet Hollywood. Ramon was a whale, and had known these men for years, during the time Las Vegas grew into the city of adult entertainment, a Disneyland for adults to play out their favorite vices. Leaving Las Vegas will give me the chance to build a real life away from the ever-controlling grip of my husband. Ramon gave me carte blanche to build a house without limits. In no time I was jumping on the jet to Beirut with the hopes of strengthening our marriage and building a dream.

We purchased the home of his ancestors, the one next to the little chapel, from his brother Joseph. We dreamed of building a castle in the sky for all our future children to enjoy and pass on from generation to generation. His business was booming in Las Vegas, so I was frequently in Lebanon working with the architect. Shannon and I worked feverishly during our days at the American Academy of Interior Design, so I was in my creative heaven, imagining the perfect house.

I'd studied interior design, and I knew how to draw plans. A lifetime in fashion gave me an expertise in fabric, color, and style. Years in Italy spent on weekend retreats near Lake Como with those fabulously wealthy playboys gave me visions of antiques, paintings, and tapestries. Visits to France filled my head with marble floors, fireplaces, and majestic columns. I wanted a European mansion like the houses of *The Great Gatsby* perched on a cliff in Newport, Rhode Island. Perhaps a house like William Randolph Hearst's San Simeon in California would be ideal in this rural mountain setting. Opulent and functional.

I bought books with photos filled with mansions, chateaux, and palaces, studying them like I was preparing a thesis. Our initial design of five-thousand square feet quickly blossomed to ten-thousand, then twenty-thousand, then forty-thousand square feet. Every trip Ramon made to check on the progress resulted in the buying more land and changing the design. In this case, bigger was better: raising the roof, adding another floor, a cinema, parking for thirty cars, and a pool with a patio for two hundred. We were building for generations.

I may have married Mr. DeSage in Las Vegas, but Debra DeSage, now thirty-eight years old, had no real friends, no children, no career, and a husband she was afraid to be around. It was time to start a new chapter as Debra Abi-Rached in a new country and build a new life. His name changed at Ellis Island years ago gave us two identities, two passports, and two countries. I was going to become a Sheika and live like a queen.

Chapter Ten

Twins

I married at thirty-seven for the right reasons. I wanted a partner, a life filled with children. Ramon was Catholic and Middle Eastern, and desperately wanted a family. My biological clock was ticking. We'd been together for two years, spending my time between our home in Las Vegas and supervising the construction of our new home in Lebanon. We were trying, but I wasn't getting pregnant. An enormous palace was under construction, with no children.

As the oldest of three siblings, my sisters and I grew up close, sharing clothes, talking about our dreams, and feeling like kindred spirits. I left home at seventeen and my two sisters married at eighteen, in a way to ease the burden on my mom. Diane wanted a life with children, baking cookies and living in a farmhouse surrounded by a white picket fence. She had no problems getting pregnant and having three children. Shannon, more of an urban hippie, wanted life in the city with a balance between a career and Mr. Right. She'd been unable to conceive and now neither could I. Fertility problems.

Mom had miscarried several times and was prescribed a drug called Stilbestrol. This was a synthetic estrogen technically named diethylstilbestrol, widely prescribed soon after the horrors of thalidomide birth defects in babies in the 1950s. Taking the drug, she was able to conceive all three of us. The medical community didn't know at that time Stilbestrol could cause infertility in her offspring, and now thirty years later we couldn't get pregnant. Shannon was also diagnosed with a rare blood disorder that could be caused by this drug, and she chose to adopt an amazing son. My sisters had children, and now it was my turn.

Before Ramon, I'd envisioned a jet-set lifestyle, filled with glamor and travel. With Ramon, everything changed. Now I imagined a life filled with children, dogs, and laughter. A happy home. I'd never taken pregnancy seriously, or the fact that it could be difficult. Now thirty-eight, I had to act quickly on whatever solutions were available to conceive.

My doctor initially prescribed a medicine called Clomid, which produces eggs and increases the rate of fertility. We also discovered Ramon had slow swimming sperm, making it difficult for the sperm to penetrate the egg. Add erectile dysfunction and a big ego to the mix, and suddenly our home was littered with Playboy magazines and subscriptions to xxx rated television channels. It drove me crazy. I was hot enough.

We tried unsuccessfully for a year to conceive. The process wasn't easy because I was traveling to Lebanon so often. Next option. It was the early nineties and fertility solutions were still very experimental. A few test tube babies had been born and scandals about doctors donating their own sperm unknowingly to women desperately trying to get pregnant. A few clinics were shut down and doctors' licenses suspended for unorthodox practices.

My clock was ticking. Tick-tock. I felt desperate. I chose to freeze embryos, the fertilized eggs, in test tubes, feeling like a pioneer. At the time one could freeze sperm, but not eggs. Eggs had to be fertilized. It was also illegal for any kind of embryo sex selection. Society was afraid only boys would be selected. China had a law only permitting one child. Female embryos were being aborted or killed. Personally, I didn't care if I had boys or girls, I just wanted a family.

I started on a routine of hormones and a cocktail of other drugs to produce a lot of eggs. Each morning, I injected my thigh with a little needle the size of a pin, filled with a clear, cold solution called Lupron. Making eggs, the less organic version. After one month, my hormones were raging, and I was crying over the smallest things.

Ramon, screamed at me, "You better fucking get pregnant, that's why I married you!" That was making it worse.

I wanted children badly; I cried even more.

The day before egg retrieval, I had to inject myself with this thick substance called human growth hormone, or HGH. It caused the eggs to ripen, ready for extraction. This time a big needle delivered the drug, leaving a bruise. I did this all alone with no help, practicing on an orange. Jamming this big needle into my butt hurt like hell.

The following morning it was time to retrieve. I was given a spinal tap to withstand what was to come next. Fully awake, I watched the monitor as the doctor inserted a long needle up through my uterus and into the ripe ovaries. Twenty eggs were extracted, the full syringes laid next to me. The eggs were placed in a petri dish. Ramon was doing his part with the help of erotic magazines in the room next door. Not a very romantic way to conceive. Sterile.

Lab technicians scooped up the sperm into needles and injected them into the eggs. We waited for a few days until the fertilized eggs divide into eight cells. One, two, four, eight. Process. Methodical. Science. Three to five embryos were frozen per test tube. To get me ready for implantation, more hormones were injected. A test tube of embryos was inserted, and the waiting began. Two weeks later, negative. So much time, money, and emotions. I was devastated. I was approaching forty. Tick-tock. Losing those precious embryos, my options were now dwindling. Mom and my sisters were supportive, but Ramon wasn't so understanding. He wanted results, like his business transactions. I felt alone, again, heavy shoulders.

We decided that rather than risking the loss of any more embryos in me, we would search for a surrogate. This was very new territory in the nineties. The doctor recommended a lawyer and we found a married woman in her twenties with two children who wanted to help. Both she and her husband signed the legal documents, legally becoming our incubator. She'd have no rights to the child, or children, and would simply carry to full term. It was not her biological child, it was ours. A fee was agreed upon. It was a fair exchange, a transaction.

Wanting to manifest twin girls, I found a magazine ad showing twins, and I framed it. It sat it next to my bedside table. Every day the picture smiled at me. I was dreaming of my future with a large, beautiful family. Ramon wanted a boy. I would be thrilled no matter what.

The surrogate conceived right away and soon after the ultrasound showed twins. Pregnant.

Ramon was thrilled, but being Catholic he still couldn't accept the fact his wife was not carrying his children. What was wrong with me anyway?

I was traveling back and forth to Lebanon frequently, wanting to share this joy with his family. I was realizing Lebanon was still very backwards in a lot of ways, and accepting modern day fertility treatments was one of them. It was probably the devil at work. If a wife could not produce children she was cast away and divorced, bringing shame on the family. I thought it was a silly, stupid idea, but I agreed to wear a pillow under my clothes for my entire pregnancy. In this modern, transparent world, I was doing the opposite, preferring to please my husband and keep the peace. Every two weeks, the pillow got slightly bigger. I never told my mom the truth. Smoke and mirrors. Charade. Happy and sad.

During the pregnancy, I shared with other women in Lebanon that I used a fertility doctor. In Las Vegas and Lebanon women would pull me aside, asking what to do. They were afraid their husbands would divorce them if they couldn't produce. I was constantly amazed at how women feared their husbands and the uncertainty of their own future if they couldn't please their man. They were afraid he would leave them old, penniless, and humiliated. A woman without a child. I never feared Ramon would leave me if I didn't conceive, but I was willing to look at fertility options. Adoption was not an option for us, and we were able to consult with the best doctors. Blessings and heartache.

This world is not at its best when a woman fears her husband, the man she sleeps next to at night. So many women are afraid of losing the security of marriage, even if it is with a man they do not love, feeling life was not worth living if they had to rely on themselves alone, fearing independence. I knew I always had myself, always had a choice. Always had an option. Always had tomorrow. Always.

Wearing my pillow, I attended all the doctor appointments with the surrogate, shopped for maternity clothes. She was saving up the money to buy a home, so we spent time together house hunting. Our palace in Lebanon was nearing completion. We furnished a nursery, hiring two nannies, a cook, and a housekeeper. Tick-tock.

On April 16, 1996, Jacqueline and Alexandra were born.

They were named after Jacqueline Kennedy and Princess Alexandra from a Grace Kelly movie called *The Swan*. My two little girls were going to live in a palace. Their names sounded international and would suit them in life, whether they lived in New York, Paris, or Beirut. I was thinking ahead.

I was in the operating room during their birth, wearing the hospital bracelet to match the foot bracelet of my two little angels. Ramon, even though his father had been a doctor, was afraid of hospitals and chose not to be there. He might faint if there was any blood. I was the first woman in this hospital to have a child by in-vitro fertilization, IVF, and the nurses were a little unclear as to how to proceed. There was a lot of red tape—the birth mother was classified as the incubator and legally not allowed to hold the children without my permission. The surrogate had no legal claim now or in the future. During the past few months, we'd become friends, and I loved her for what she was doing. I wanted to share the excitement. Two mothers, two children. Beautiful.

Jacky came out first, eyes wide open, a curious soul and so beautiful. I felt the true joy of the birth of my first child. Alex came out five minutes later, eyes still closed and wanting to go back to sleep. I wanted her to look at me and see this new world. I waited and waited and now had two little girls for the rest of my life. Twins! Ramon was excited, as was my mom. She was going to accompany me back to Lebanon and stay awhile, helping with our two new little girls. She was amazed at how quickly I returned to my pre-pregnancy figure. Secrets.

My big, amazing house was almost finished, and we were ready to fill it with kids. After so many trips back and forth, we were now nearing completion of forty-thousand square feet of living space plus another forty-thousand square feet of garage, pool, and guest quarters. It had evolved into an enormous palace. I was speaking beginner French and trying to learn Arabic, so I could communicate with the Syrian or Kurdish laborers and the Lebanese contractor, able to get a ladder moved or order lunch. It took four years to build this home. I was ready to return to Beirut with my two babies, to start a new chapter in life.

Ramon was busy in Vegas, and the surrogate agreed to start on a second in-vitro fertilization procedure, needing more money for their home. Hopefully there would be a boy this time since this was still

Ramon's quest. I needed to get back to Beirut. There was furniture to buy, gardens to plant, and a palace to run. Even then I had this gut feeling I was creating an opulent prison for myself instead of a happy home. A fabulous adventure or doom and gloom? One step in front of the other.

I spent my time shopping for furniture and antiques, decorating an eighty-thousand-foot palace. In Lebanon, we hired a full-time nanny at two hundred and a chauffeur at three hundred dollars a month. Taking twenty employees to manage the palace. The chauffeur drove me from our village Bejdarfel to Beirut, one hour away, while my nannies constantly watched my girls. Two months later our surrogate called, pregnant again! It was strange, I wasn't even there and we were pregnant. Twins for a second time, but this time I was losing the pillow. I'd had enough of that charade.

This long winding road of an adventure was taking shape, and my amazing dream home was going to be filled with children. I moved into our palace we named, Chateau St. Antoine, because of the little chapel of the Abi-Rached clan. I was living this wonderful adventure but without a husband, next to me. Would he ever come back to his country of birth? Would he ever appreciate and enjoy this beautiful dream we talked about so long? Would he ever want to enjoy being a husband and father to a wonderful family that wanted to love him?

He was the Lebanese immigrant living amongst the brightest lights of Las Vegas, while I was the American blonde bombshell living in the remote village of Bejdarfel, in the mountains of the Phoenicians. The ancient and the modern. Two worlds apart.

Chapter Eleven

Life in the Palace

It was early 1997. I was living life at the top, jetting between Beirut and Las Vegas three or four times a year. The second surrogacy was successful, and we were waiting for Dominique and Christina to be born in June. Our magnificent Chateau St. Antoine soon would safekeep four daughters. I was ecstatic. Ramon was still yearning for a boy, wanting to carry on the family name and his legacy. I was doing my best, having no way to order a boy. I hoped his daughters would make him happy, and perhaps reconnect him to me and his beloved Lebanon.

Four years spent dreaming of this palatial home and we went over the top, purchasing books on grand palaces, villas, and the chateaux of Europe for inspiration. The architect and I decided on a collaboration of ideas from San Simeon in California to Chateau de Fontainebleau outside of Paris. We needed large reception areas for entertaining and an enormous family kitchen, and of course lots of bedrooms.

Our home was built on the highest point near the center of the village. Driving up the road, one could see the large entrance gates with enormous palm trees flanking each side. Cars paused outside while the security guards verified their identity. The enormous bronze gates stood fourteen feet high, guarding our family. Cars proceeded through the porte cochere, whose arched ceiling was filled with carved plaster moldings and intricate florets. Stone cobblestones and mosaic paving reminiscent of Phoenician times were intricately laid throughout the plaza ahead.

The vast courtyard contained potted planters lined with date palms and gardenias, leading toward an enormous water fountain styled after Central Park in New York. We found an identical copy in Las Vegas, shipping it to Beirut along with dozens of garden sculptures. The finished chateau was forty-thousand square feet above ground and another forty-thousand unseen from the entrance. Stones quarried from the mountains above Beirut were hand-chipped and formed to give the appearance of a villa built two hundred years prior, everything oversized. The exterior stonework took five years to install, as every rock, column, and window molding was handmade.

The Palladian windows and doors were made of solid wood and beveled glass, all opening out to marble terraces checkered in beige and white. Interior support columns were solid yellow marble imported from Italy to coordinate with the marble flooring. Beautiful marble inlay designs copied from Venetian palaces were strategically placed throughout the entrance and hallways. All the crown moldings throughout were a foot deep and gilded with 24-karat gold leaf. The wood carvings on the ten-foot interior doors were also gilded. There were six grand carved marble fireplaces, a four-story bronze staircase with gold rail, and thirty-two bathrooms. I called this home, pinching myself. It was perfect for entertaining with grand reception rooms, yet having wonderful spaces for family life, kids and dogs.

Buying antiques was fun! I found Flemish and French tapestries twenty feet long, dating back to the sixteenth century. Gilt bronze chandeliers dripping with foot-long crystal pendants were hung from the fifteen-foot ceilings. Many of the crystals had been found in Paris, some of them coming from Versailles. Master paintings, Russian icons, and vases from Sevres were everywhere. My favorite objects were the beautiful carpets from Iran: handmade Tabriz floor coverings in bold colors of yellow, blue, red, and turquoise. I loved the hand-knotted carpets with animal and flower motifs.

I found a creative soulmate in an artist named Naji Chartouni, spending months creating custom furniture, wall décor, and objects to give the palace a true renaissance feel. Naji and I researched every detail of these grand furniture designs, creating oversized reception tables, velvet covered chairs, and enormous gilded mirrors. Later, he made multiple copies of our collaborative efforts and sold them to the kings and emirs throughout the Middle East. We loved baroque, opulence, and over the top grandiose. When intermixing the newly created pieces with museum quality antiques, the result was awe inspiring.

It was a palace to entertain, having parties at the pool for three hundred guests. Everyone hoped for an invitation. We had a jazz band or four-piece classic ensemble to play for our gatherings by the pool, inviting violinists to play in our Arabic salon for more intimate events. We consumed lobsters by the dozen, drinking champagne by the case, living the life of Gatsby. Valet attendants parked the cars of ambassadors, politicians, and the shady rich. I never asked who they were or how they earned their money. It was just dinner for god's sake.

All of this opulence came with a price. Our first home in Las Vegas cost two million dollars. I envisioned spending ten million dollars on this second home in Lebanon, simply a pied a terre for infrequent visits. Four years and hundreds of changes later pushed the expenditures of this palace to over thirty million. Ramon was giving me carte blanche, never having a budget. I built a mini-Versailles.

Running a palace in a third-world country should be inexpensive, as we were in a village, not even a town. It was still post-war Lebanon and the infrastructure of the country had not been rebuilt. We were constantly without power, phones, and water. Forget having a freezer. The power went on and off so much, everything would melt. I never had an electric clock, instead learning to use battery powered everything.

Diesel generators were installed to run our elevators, lights, and garden needs, essentially everything. The fuel costs were running about two thousand per month, and another two thousand monthly for the electric power that was spotty. And then there was the gasoline.

We installed our own ten-thousand-gallon tank in the garage, costing twenty thousand dollars every time to fill. Of course, all our employees and relatives considered this free for their cars. It was amazing how frequently we had to fill the tank.

All this space came with enormous maintenance, and I'd had no idea a big lifestyle came with such big expenses. It wasn't part of the Cinderella calculus. It was now.

Our garage had space for about twenty-five cars needing chauffeurs and a mechanic. Usually, we had eight nannies to cook, clean, and watch the kids. All were from the Philippines, speaking perfect English. We needed four gardeners to manage the two acres of manicured grounds and another twenty acres of olive trees. We grew our own vegetables. The vast majority were stolen by migrant workers in the area.

We had thousands of olive trees covering the hills around our palace. It was a tradition for hundreds of years for the villagers to plow and fertilize the rugged ground, waiting for the October olive harvest. Coincidentally, the olives ripened and were ready to pick when the tribes of the Bedouins passed through our village, all their possessions packed on donkeys, stuffed to the brim with carpets, cooking pans, and clothing. They laid blankets on the ground and beat the olive trees with sticks until the olives dropped and the branches were bare. As payment, they took half the harvest, giving me the other half. I took my share to the local monastery for the monks to cold press the olives into virgin olive oil. Again, they kept half. I still ended up with enough oil to feed an army, though it cost a fortune to fertilize and maintain the groves.

On occasion, the Bedouins, arriving early at night without notice, stole all the olives. It was too much to handle and too much space to control. Not wanting to hire security for the groves, I delegated the entire operation to the local farmers, ending up with a few barrels of oil at the end of each year. I had what I needed, and the farmers were all productive. Happy home.

Security was a priority in the village. I was an American citizen living in the Middle East with my kids, without a husband nearby. Ramon was spending most of his time in Las Vegas, leaving me to manage the house.

Through the American Embassy, I met their chief of security, who by coincidence had a fiancée living in our village. Visiting frequently, he would oversee our security operations, installing cameras inside and out and hiring three teams of guards for around-the-clock security. A collection of AK-47s and Glocks, along with night vision goggles were on hand. I always had an entourage close by that was fully armed. I built a safe room constructed of walls two feet thick and a bulletproof steel door for emergencies. A piercing alarm alerted the police if we were under duress, giving us time to hide when necessary. We did everything possible to feel safe. The US Embassy constantly warned us of the dangers close by.

My situation seemed scarier on CNN than in real life, but you could never predict what could happen. Though my village of Bejdarfel was peaceful and in the Christian area of the north, the radical groups Hezbollah, Hamas, and even Al Qaeda were operating not too far from my house.

I never felt like a target, but this girl from Seattle felt safer by taking extreme precaution, having two, armed chauffeur/bodyguards with me and two with my children at all times.

Living in Beirut was like living in a miniature capsule of world society. Each country being represented by their ambassador or consulate, hosting fabulous parties for all the social players of the day. The best parties were at the French or Spanish Embassies, big palaces built in the eighteen hundreds, filled with a mix of antiques from their respective country and ancient museum-quality relics of the Phoenicians. Combine the international flavor of visiting dignitaries with the corrupt politicians of the Middle East and you have this decadent atmosphere similar to British India in the nineteen twenties.

I adapted well to this international way of life. My days were spent with my two babies at home and managing our palace. I managed it like a hotel with a large staff. I had bills to pay and lawyers to help me with legalities over some of the lands we bought. Ramon's two brothers didn't want me in the picture, feeling like I was a threat to their lifelong hold on their younger brother. I tried to keep our village business separate from the brothers, but Ramon always found a way to complicate matters without my knowing, leaving me in the dark. The three of them considered me a problem, never giving me credit for a job well done.

My evenings were spent playing dress up. There were so many parties and dinners to attend, I could only choose the best two or three each week. Ramon was never with me, his business always keeping him in Las Vegas. Beirut was overflowing with widows and lonely wives of prominent businessmen who were also never in the country. These "cache" of ladies were always seated at the same table, showing off spectacular jewelry and Judith Lieber gem-encrusted handbags, gossiping and making excuses for the absence of our husbands. I was one of them, fitting right in.

The most opulent parties were given by my friend Angelique Chartouni, who had a big beautiful house for entertaining. Entering the foyer, there was a live orchestra and servants handing you flutes of champagne. It was always black-tie, RSVP, meaning long dresses and the biggest jewels you had. Originally from Brazil, her emeralds were the size of walnuts, her rubies larger than acorns, and tiers upon tiers of diamonds. Buffet tables were piled high with caviar and foie gras, seating tables laden with sterling silver and flickering candles. Guests seated at round tables of eight in covered loggias overlooked the lighted gardens. Dinner service started at ten at night and lasted until three in the morning. No one wanted to leave.

Her party's guests list included visiting royalty from Europe and politicians from the past and present. Throw in a few business tycoons and the parties were a real who's who. She invited me all the time because I made an effort to wear amazing long dresses and fabulous jewelry, and I love to dance. After dinner she and I broke the ice by inviting someone else's husband to dance. Angelique was nearly ninety years old. This was Beirut's society. You never knew when war would break out, so you lived in the moment, to the extremes. And yet, I was alone, again.

I'd lived in Milan, New York, Los Angeles, and Las Vegas — sophisticated cities. But nowhere else did I experience the high society ambience of Beirut. You forgot the political turmoil when you entered the grandiose doors of palace court. Decadent fun. I felt blessed for being so immersed in Lebanese society.

At the same time, it was a paradox. The country depicted on CNN was so far removed from the one I was living in. Beirut on TV was war, skirmishing militias, riots in the streets, and constant dangers.

I was living in a world of chauffeurs and champagne. I knew danger was imminent, but always had the ability to hop on a plane to Paris, to wait out the problems of this third-world country. Then I would return as soon as possible to this delicious life.

Chapter Twelve
Dual Lives

I was living with my staff and my two daughters in Lebanon in the spring of 1997. It was a short trip to Las Vegas to be present for the birth of my next twins, Dominique and Christina. I was enjoying life in Beirut, although I needed to come back to America. Ramon was still living and working in Las Vegas, wanting to try one more time for a son. Returning to Vegas was a culture shock, re-entering the world of gambling, deal-making, and Ramon's extremely dominating personality.

Ramon constantly showed me how radical his thinking was and how another opinion was never allowed in any conversation. He was adamant in his belief O.J. Simpson would never kill Nicole Brown Simpson, flying into a rage when I expressed my opposite thoughts on the matter. The US presidential campaign between Bob Dole and Bill Clinton gave me another glimpse into Ramon's character. He was taking thousand-dollar checks from his employees and reimbursing them with cash. I knew the limitations for individuals making campaign contributions was one thousand dollars per person and Ramon already made the contribution on our behalf. He was trying to be a bigshot for Bob Dole, contributing illegally.

"Ramon, you can't reimburse your employees, it's illegal."

"Shut your fucking mouth, it's none of your business!"

Ramon met a local politician named Hal Furman who was running on the Republican ticket and was being supported by Bob Dole. I greatly admired Bob Dole and his wife Elizabeth. We met Bob at a small private party in the home of Steve Wynn. Ramon, wanting to support Bob and Hal, offered to do fundraising. Of course, neither of them said no. So, Ramon started to send checks, lots of checks. I guess Ramon thought no one would notice nearly all the checks were from his employees. Several years passed, and Ramon was investigated by the federal government, charged with illegal campaign contributions and ordered to pay one hundred seventy-five thousand dollars in fines and he made a twenty-five-thousand-dollar charitable contribution to the Catholic Charities of Southern Nevada. It was his first federal offense. He wouldn't listen.

I really thought he lived life on the edge, that he was successful and business was booming. He was still gambling every night, and entertaining presidents of major cosmetic and perfume companies, showing them Las Vegas like they never imagined. When we were seated at dinner, Ramon would arrive and tell us how lucky he had been at the tables, throwing ten-thousand-dollar bundles of cash to his clients, their eyes popping out of their heads.

Ramon loved live boxing events usually held at the MGM Grand or outdoors at Caesar's Palace. It was the only time he left the gaming tables for fun. We were in the front row when Mike Tyson bit the ear off of Evander Holyfield. Our thousand-dollar seats were next to Donald Trump, Tom Cruise, and Nicole Kidman. My sister Shannon and her husband joined us for this event, making reservations after the fight at an Italian restaurant just outside the arena with a view of the casino floor.

The opening bell rang, and immediately Tyson bit Holyfield's ear. Referee Mills Lane stopped the fight, and should have disqualified Tyson, but a twenty-million-dollar purse was at hand and HBO needed to keep the show going. The fight resumed, and Tyson bit Holyfield's other ear. The fight was stopped, blood everywhere. The audience exited the arena, a wave of rap stars and celebrities moving tightly and together out of the arena and into the gaming area.

Arriving at the restaurant, Shannon and I sat down. I picked up my glass of wine and gunshots rang out. I dove under the table, not

Chapter Thirteen

Mona

Traditions in Lebanon run deep, especially in the villages outside metropolitan Beirut. Politicians win elections if they show up at funerals, marriages, and baptisms. We were building a family and somehow running in these political circles, so Ramon was doing favors for everyone wanting to get elected. I think somewhere in his Maronite Catholic upbringing, he had a desire to someday become president. Also at the same time, he was trying to establish a business in Lebanon. Post-war Beirut had opportunities everywhere: cell phones, real estate, downtown reconstruction, gas, and electricity. He started importing containers of goods from the US through his business Cadeau Express—the French version of gift express. Initially it was fifty containers with crystal, China, perfume, watches, and anything else he could get a good deal on.

He acquired an enormous warehouse where the goods were received, priced, and then opened to the public. It was located in the city of Jounieh, next to the Casino du Liban. There was no advertising, only word of mouth brought the customers running. And the containers kept on arriving.

Reconstruction was now at full speed in downtown Beirut and Elias Haroui was the newly elected president. Rafik Hariri was prime minister, and Nabil Berri was speaker of the house. Ramon befriended the new president and his wife, Mona, with offers of donations — in particular the Presidential Palace, the Red Cross, and the rebuilding of the Museum of Beirut. Mona was establishing a hospital called the Chronic Care Center and needed money and equipment. Having so much merchandise coming from the US, Ramon invited her to come and look at what we had on hand and perhaps she could use something. She arrived the following day with two trucks and a platoon of Lebanese soldiers, loading up pallet after pallet. She took a lot, to say the least, and in return started inviting us frequently to the Presidential Palace for lunch and dinner.

Arriving for lunch, our four-car entourage drove through heavily guarded gates, past the armed guards and checkpoints. A huge modern palace stood before us with twenty-foot arches lining the façade, and everything was covered in white marble. We drove through the porte cochere to be escorted by uniformed security personnel through metal detectors and into the office of the president. His personal office was very large and decorated in dark mahogany and polished crème marble. Ancient Phoenician statues rested on columns of stone and fresh pink lilies were on all the tables. The president spoke English rather well, but French was the language of business. We spoke briefly about politics in general, and of our hopes for the children of Lebanon. After thirty minutes, he took me by the hand and lead us into a small private elevator from his office to the floor above.

The second floor was the presidential residence. There was polished crème marble strewn with antique Caucasian carpets and collections of more Phoenician stone statues. There were no paintings, rather Kilim rugs and ceramic mosaics decorated the walls. Fresh flowers were everywhere, and it smelled like a garden. The dining room was decorated in an English style with a long dark wood formal table and Chippendale chairs. An enormous Venetian crystal chandelier hung brightly over a handmade tablecloth embroidered with blue flowers in the same design as the China. Glassware was cut crystal from St. Louis, the best French crystal maker in the world, and our flatware was solid silver. I sat on the president's left, Mona on his right, and Ramon next to Mona. The conversation was light and jovial, no talk of politics at lunch, as was customary in Lebanon.

After dessert and Turkish coffee, the President excused himself and left back through his private elevator.

Mona took us on a private tour of their personal residence: a huge salon for her family, a large kitchen, and of course her closet — rows and rows of Dior, Escada, Chanel, Lebanese designers Elie Saab, George Chakra, and Zuhair Mrad. She had exquisite taste. We talked about her charities while she escorting us back to our waiting cars. Ramon scratched a check for twenty-five thousand dollars, promising more. This invitation was repeated frequently. On occasion they invited us to bring our girls. Four little girls won the president's heart, and he spent an hour with them taking pictures and making them laugh.

Mona started bringing her trucks and soldiers to every shipment. Ramon, unknowingly to me, purchased a vintage Rolls-Royce convertible as a surprise gift for me, only to find out later that it ended up in the garage of the president. Ramon was very generous when making a donation to the Red Cross. Twelve fully equipped ambulances were shipped directly to the Presidential Palace. A staged media event was coordinated to announce the donation. An entire marching band of soldiers and uniformed guards saluted the caravan of outfitted Dodge ambulances. I was never more-proud of giving away money.

Ramon was teaching Mona how to buy gifts and resell for a profit, showing her how to stock her gift shop at the hospital, and inviting her society friends for Easter or Christmas shopping, raising money for the hospital and walking out with nicely wrapped gift baskets. She was inviting everyone: sheiks, emirs, politicians, and rich Middle Eastern wives. Mona was smart, and she raised a lot of money. She showed her gratitude by inviting me and several women for the afternoon to swim and have lunch in her fragrant gardens.

Mona loved to entertain with the grandest style, unforgettable evenings. Normally there were three hundred people, all formally dressed. You were chauffeured to the entrance where the uniformed valets opened your car door as you stepped onto red carpets. This would be an occasion to show off your emeralds or diamonds and how generous your husband was to you. In Beirut, there were so many formal parties. The Lebanese parliament of about two hundred ministers and deputies was perhaps the richest elected government in the world, having all found a way to profit from their positions, sometimes legally and sometimes not. I was not going to judge any of them on how they made their money, it was just dinner and I was a guest. We were laughing and making jokes in three languages, sometimes all languages in one sentence.

We dined, listened to music and danced into the early hours. Sometimes a Middle Eastern diva would sing, or perhaps a European tenor. Entertainment ranged from Russian ballet troupes to local Arabic dancers. We partied by candlelight, champagne flowing, everyone flirting. Sometimes sitting there, seated next to the President, wondering how so much money could be spent in one evening. This was still a poor third-world country, with beggars in the street. It reminded me of Marie Antoinette and her famously quoted response when hearing her people had no bread.

"Let them eat cake."

Chapter Fourteen

Baptisms and Bishops

There was a small private chapel adjacent to our palace built for the Abi-Rached clan in the year 1904. Ramon's great uncle was a priest, presiding over this chapel for his entire life, offering refuge and sanctuary for inhabitants of the village Bejdarfel. It was named after St. Antoine de Padua, the patron saint of lost items, lost souls.

During construction of our palace, the chapel was completely refurbished, stripping the bright blue paint down to the natural original stone. It had a double vaulted ceiling and a raised altar for the priest. The Abi-Rached family would use this chapel for weddings, baptisms, and funerals, squeezing in forty to fifty people in the twenty or so pews. Our first cousin, Khairellah Abi-Rached, lived across the fence and next to his brother Majid. They were my closest neighbors, and they taught me a lot about tradition. It was tradition that only the Abi-Rached clan could be buried at the chapel. Only men or the spinster women, keeping the name alive and untainted. We shared the chapel with the family, respecting family needs.

The first time I witnessed a family funeral was a bit of a culture shock. Khairellah came from a family of eight. He was the oldest, raising his younger siblings. His elderly aunt had just passed away.

She would be buried within the chapel, having died unmarried. Before the burial the body was lying in state at Khairellah's house on a refrigerated table in the living room surrounded by women praying and crying loudly. The men were at a different home, praying for her safe passage. The body was dressed in lovely clothes, arms crossed, and flowers placed close to her.

The men would carry the casket during the funeral procession, following the church choir led by the priest. The men lifted her up and lowered her into the casket, carrying it above their heads throughout the procession to the chapel. The mass was performed by a visiting bishop and then her casket was carried into the lower-level mausoleum. I'd never seen a dead body so up close and personal. This village's heartbeat revolved around birth, marriage, death, and the church. The priests were busy.

As Sheika of our village, and to be a part of the Abi-Rached clan, baptizing my four daughters in the church was vital. It was 1998 and they were less than two years old, and the villagers let me know it was time. Aware of how to throw a party, that was the easy part, but a local traditional baptism was a learning experience. Khairellah helped me locate three bishops to preside over the ceremony, with their tall dramatic ceremonial headdresses. I loved the richness of their brightly jewel-colored robes, heavily embroidered to match the enormous, pointed hats. Their golden religious jewelry added to the effect. Filling the chapel with flowers and candles created a regal spectacle, while honoring the spiritual essence. We invited the entire Abi-Rached clan along with our high-profile friends for an unforgettable occasion.

Ramon arrived a week prior to the ceremony on the Gulfstream IV. The president and Madame Mona Harouri would be attending. Mona agreed to be godmother for this important occasion. My two sisters flew in with their husbands from Seattle. Mom was there, of course. Caterers, florists, waiters, and well-wishers buzzing about in a circus of joy. I did well in these moments, waving my magic wand and having it all come together.

The guest list surpassed two-hundred for the baptism followed by a lunch in our palace. Valet attendants were furiously parking cars when the president's motorcade arrived. I stopped inside the entrance, waiting for the soldiers with machine guns to jump out of the escort vehicle. They looked like Secret Service with dark sunglasses and walkie-talkies, standing at attention for the president of Lebanon. President Elias was wearing a white suit, while Mona was wearing an elegant pink suit. My girls were wearing pink organza dresses, and I chose Oscar de la Renta completely beaded and covered in pastel silk flowers.

After all the guests arrived, we paraded up the stone stairs to the chapel, entering through the side door and gathering in front of the stately bishops. Grand and regal in their ornate robes and chanting in Latin, they blessed our daughters with scepters like a scene from a Da Vinci painting. Mona signed the chapel book as godmother and my girls were now officially Maronite Catholic.

We were eating, drinking, and partying for hours. Mona, my two sisters, and I positioned ourselves at the dessert table to cut the cakes, each taking a ceremonial knife to the Barbie Doll cakes while champagne corks popped. It was a moment to remember. The president and Mona kissed us all goodbye. With a regal flourish, the car doors closed and the motorcade then zoomed away. Ramon, saving the best for last, led me into his office and presented me with a sixteen-carat yellow diamond ring, square shaped, with two triangle diamonds in the setting.

"This is for the girls."

We embraced. I felt a flickering moment of love and respect.

There were still times in our marriage where Ramon and I were on the same page. I called him daily from Lebanon, usually in my morning which was his evening. I knew his schedule. He would be finishing at the office and on his way to the casinos. Most of the time this was when he was in his best mood, and I shared with him the moments I spent with the girls or updated him on the current situation in the country. I never knew if he was truly interested. I learned not to take it personally. Spinning emotional plates. Keeping the show going.

I really wanted to love him and have him love me back. We were building a wonderful life together, having so much potential to live happily ever after. He was amazingly smart with a gift of charm and everyone wanted to do business with him, both in Las Vegas and in Beirut. Couldn't we find a way to live in this palace, happily? So many opportunities exist in every domain. I believed Las Vegas was a cesspool of temptation that eventually would lead to the downfall of my husband.

We had gone through in vitro twice and were lucky to have four beautiful daughters. Our family abided by local tradition and the girls were now baptized in the church. I was doing everything to earn my title as a Sheika in our tiny village. I was still hoping my Sheik would find happiness. But I knew my husband would never be happy until he could celebrate having a son. Traditions and heritage dictated you had to produce a male heir.

Prior to baptizing our girls, we set in motion a third attempt at conceiving a boy. We located another surrogate, and implantation was successful. We knew it was going to be twins again, but I was nervously waiting to find out what gender. Either way, I would be the luckiest girl in the world. With Ramon, however, I was afraid he would lash out at me for not producing his son. Nothing else mattered.

I accompanied him to the tarmac the day following the baptism, hugging and kissing him goodbye. It was bittersweet, spending time this summer in his homeland in our wonderful home surrounded by friends and family. Why couldn't it always be like this? As he climbed the jet stairs, I wondered when I would see him next. It may be a day or a year, whatever was convenient for him.

I waved goodbye.

Returned to my fairytale life, looking for a happy ending.

My heart knew differently.

Chapter Fifteen
This Jet is Too Small

Ramon always traveled by private jet, usually leasing one from his friend Ralph Englestad, who owned the Imperial Palace Casino on the strip in Las Vegas. Ralph was also one of Ramon's investors, living right up the street from us close to Wayne Newton's estate. Within the casino Ralph had a world-class car collection like no other. Perhaps two hundred vintage and collector cars displayed in a grand exhibition arena showcasing Duesenberg, Ferraris, and Rolls Royce. He owned the cars of Bonnie and Clyde, Hitler, Elvis, and John F. Kennedy. He also owned a Gulfstream IV and a Boeing 727 that he kept in a private hangar at McCarran Airport.

It was really expensive flying private, costing perhaps two-hundred-fifty-thousand dollars per trip between Las Vegas and Beirut. Ramon made the trip only once per year, but I was still traveling commercial with four kids, four nannies, and my mom. We traveled coach, as I wanted to sit with my kids, and we could bring so much more luggage on a commercial flight. Returning from Vegas, I sometimes checked more than thirty suitcases packed with goods. Lebanon was still a third-world country, and I needed bath towels, plastic glassware, and kid's clothes from America. I may be living in a palace, but I needed basic necessities I could only find at Walmart.

I expected to travel mid-October of 1998 and await the birth of our third set of twins. I was ecstatic about two more girls, Sabrina and Tiffany. I must have been thinking of Audrey Hepburn when choosing these names. Ramon was disappointed in not manifesting a son, but happy we now had a rather large family. Ramon called on October third: "I'm a dad!" The twins arrived early, so I missed the birth.

Crazy. I was half-way around the world and not needing to be there for the birth of my children. I flew out the next day with four children, six nannies, and two double strollers. The framed photo of the twin girls still displayed at my bedside table proved manifestation worked. I was taking this trip less often as my life revolved around raising our children in Lebanon, and Ramon was still actively working and gambling in Las Vegas. As his wife, I still hoped someday we would live together in a normal family environment and he would see these wonderful children grow up.

We arrived at LAX International Airport and went straight to the hospital where my two newborns were in incubators. They were nearly three weeks early but weighed over four pounds each. My mom was there and Ramon oohed and awed at how cute they were. They looked so fragile I was afraid of picking them up. Their little legs were smaller than my thumb. The hospital did not allow them to come home until they weighed over five pounds. I breathed a sigh of relief grateful the nurses would be caring for them for the next ten days. Cautious.

We checked into a nearby hotel, booking four rooms, Ramon returning to Vegas. He left us a twelve-passenger van for my kids, nannies, and luggage. And now I had a new role, chauffeur. I desired some fun for the next ten days before picking-up Sabrina and Tiffany: Applebee's, Walmart, water parks, and zoos, before gathering all six girls and heading to Las Vegas.

My mind raced, thinking deeply about my marriage. Ramon lived in one country and I lived half-way around the world in another. He was difficult, but he was still my husband, and our marriage was sure to crumble if we couldn't find the time to be together. Analyzing our options, we discussed our marriage at great length. Spending more time together at least in the summer and over the holidays was the only option remaining. Currently we were spending two weeks in the summer and two weeks at Christmas. Our three-bedroom Las Vegas home was too small, so we needed something larger for six children.

We found a teardown property next to Mike Tyson on a street called Tomiyasu, bordering a large park. Starting from scratch, again, we worked with architects to create a wonderful home for our six daughters. This was going to cost another fortune, and I was wondering where all this money was coming from. Two Rolls-Royces were parked outside, along with my new passenger van. Ramon assured me not to worry. I watched him daily count the stacks of cash from his previous night's gambling. Don't ask, don't tell. Ignorance is bliss.

I envisioned the family living together in Las Vegas for three months in the summer and another two weeks at Christmas. I'd grown to love Lebanon and the world we created. Our children would speak three languages while attending schools in Beirut, raised with an international background and making friends from all over the world. I was preparing them for a future, giving them, all the opportunities I never had while growing up in Seattle. Lebanon was home and Las Vegas was simply a vacation destination to save my marriage.

The 1998 report to Congress on the Public Integrity Section was published, naming Ramon DeSage as having violated the Federal Election Campaign Act. Not surprising, as I argued so vehemently about his breaking the law during the previous election. All violations regarded the 1996 Bob Dole campaign and the fines of two hundred thousand dollars he had to pay. I was really hoping this would be the last of his brushes with the law. Being eternally optimistic, I thought we had a chance at a happy marriage if Ramon escaped the gambling of Las Vegas and contributed to the growth and reconstruction of Lebanon. We had a palace filled with beautiful things, maids, chauffeurs, and servants for all our needs. Why should we spend another fortune on a home in Sin City?

I only planned on staying a few weeks, working with the new architect on designs to rebuild the teardown house. With so many children we needed at least six bedrooms, though I would love eight. During our visit Ramon did not join us for a family dinner or afternoon to spend time with the kids. He needed to go to the casinos at night, clients hovering in mystery, always calling for appointments. We put our three-bedroom home up for sale. Ramon was planning on moving into one of his complimentary VIP penthouse suites on the Las Vegas strip. I couldn't imagine where we would be staying on our next summer visit.

I bought another double stroller, taking the return trip with six kids, six nannies, myself, and my mom. A traveling party of fourteen. This now meant I could travel with twenty-eight pieces of luggage. Ramon offered us the Gulfstream IV, but it only held ten suitcases and twelve passengers, it was just too small. We boarded Air France, wishing Ralph would get a bigger plane.

Chapter Sixteen

Friends in High Places

Lebanon was a country divided into three religious' groups, all having equal political power. Rafik Hariri, the prime minister represented the Sunnis; Nabil Berri, speaker of the house, represented the Shiite Muslims; and Elias Haroui, the president, represented the Christians. The Shiite have support from Iran, while the Sunni have the backing of Saudi Arabia.

In 1967 Israel invaded the southern border of Lebanon, and have been occupying it ever since. The Shiite resistance group, Hezbollah, formed at that time to stop further aggression from Israel. Politics remains a very complicated situation, as eight hundred thousand Palestinian refugees in Lebanon, mostly Sunni, are without citizenship. Granting them legal status would throw off the delicate balance of power in a country of only four million inhabitants.

Living in the Middle East, I had friends deeply involved in each tradition. I chose not to be political, making girlfriends based on joy and friendship. I lived in the Christian area close to Byblos and spent my time between Beirut to the south and Batroun to the north, rarely venturing to the southern border of Israel or Syria to the north. My girlfriends were amazing women from around the world who married

Lebanese men. I was not alone in discovering the allure of the Beirut lifestyle. We chose to live in this chaotic country for its glamor and exotic nature, knowing we have passports and visas if needing to flee. Most Lebanese yearned for the freedom to pursue life outside this country where jobs paid little and war was on every horizon.

My best friend, Marianne Helou, was from the Loire Valley in France. She was sophisticated, glamorous, smart, and loving. Her husband, Henri, was a member of parliament, following the traditions established by his father, Pierre. The family had a long involvement in Lebanese politics, going back several generations, striving for democratic reform and a prosperous Lebanon.

My other close friend, Mary Cochran, was from Baton Rouge, Louisiana. She was married to Roderick Sursolk Cochran, from one of the founding families of Lebanon. They lived in a magnificent palace in downtown Beirut, built in 1850 during the time when Lebanon was a French colony. The three of us, having lunch in Mary's Garden, spoke of design and gossiped about politics. We marveled at how Lebanon was not at all like what was portrayed on CNN. On the contrary, we had lives of privilege and comfort. Yet, we understood war could break out at any moment and our lives could change in an instant. We loved each other and equally Lebanon.

Our husbands made the laws and created the jobs. We never worried about putting food on the table or the price of gasoline. We believed we were being generous by leaving a twenty-dollar tip for a waiter that made one hundred dollars a week. Danger was everywhere, but our close-knit group remained connected to each other, introducing to each other people that we needed in order to survive.

One of these introductions was to the head of Lebanese intelligence, Jamil Sayed, who lived on a large farm in the Bekaa Valley. We would drive in an SUV caravan ranging from four to eight vehicles past the Roman temples and vast acres of vineyards. Arriving near the border of Syria, we would be greeted by a simple buffet of a Lebanese mezza. Our six daughters played with his puppies and canaries in the gardens while Ramon and Jamil discussed events in private. We always traveled with extreme security measures, more for showing off than for any real danger. A friend like Jamil could someday come in handy if any real danger ever appeared at our door.

Our bodyguards were on constant alert when opening the doors of the black SUVs. Pitch black windows to disguised who was inside.

I was always baffled how they could drive. Sitting in the back seat, I casually rested my feet on AK-47s. My two personal bodyguards spoke perfect English and were with me constantly, protecting me and my children 24/7.

Another connection required us traveling by car to Damascus to visit the Syrian vice president, Halim Haddam. Our black SUV caravan drove two hours to the Syrian border, where Ramon and I would transfer into the private car of the vice president, a heavily armored Mercedes limousine. It was more like a tank with bulletproof glass two inches thick. We sped across borders, not even stopping at the heavily fortified checkpoints. It took another thirty minutes to reach his private residence in the city.

I became fast friends with Rim, his daughter. She was elegant, extroverted, and had a great sense of fashion. Selling any goods manufactured outside Syria was strictly illegal, but of course, Rim was the daughter of the vice president and bent the rules. She had a small shop on the street just below their home where she imported top European brands. All her friends and connections were invited for tea and shopping. It was very exclusive. The ladies were downstairs shopping and gossiping while the men talked politics upstairs.

Rim's husband, Orphan, was a Syrian businessman who manufactured chocolate. He and Ramon created a company to ship Syrian chocolate back to Nevada, mini chocolate bars wrapped in gold foil to look like gold bars. The gold bars were then packaged in red velvet boxes. DeSage Chocolate was in business and containers of chocolate were shipped to Ramon's warehouses in Las Vegas.

I stayed friends with Rim for years, sometimes traveling alone to her house in Damascus so we could speak in private. Rim always sent her father's car to pick me up at the border to make my journey safer. We gossiped about the wives of politicians and the potential for war, sometimes visiting the ancient souks that were filled with carpets, Damascus fabrics embroidered with gold threads, and aisle after aisle of jewelry, both silver and gold. We would sit at a small cafe and drink the heavily sweetened tea while listening to the music of the local Arabic chanting. It was so exotic.

When I married Ramon, his father had been a Sheik, a title Ramon assumed when he returned to Lebanon. Since I was married to Ramon, I was a Sheika, a title I considered a great honor. I appreciated the respect given to me by my village neighbors and tried to adopt their customs and traditions in return, knowing their wives and children, buying gas at their stores, fixing my cars at their shops, and visiting their local cafes. We were family and I wanted to be loyal.

It took ten years to build an amazing social network of wonderful friends, entrepreneurial businessmen, and very important politicians who would take your phone call. We were invited everywhere, and our door was constantly open to the world. It was the life we had envisioned and worked so hard for. It was the life we spoke of on our first date at café Roma so long ago in Beverly Hills. We realized our dream of wealth, success, and family; we had it all.

But Ramon was spending less and less time in our perfect cocoon, preferring the clatter of the slot machines and the bright lights of Las Vegas. I was morphing into the socialite in the spotlight, always looking for my partner.

Chapter Seventeen
Life Changing Events

I was so grateful for our six healthy, happy girls, always frolicking about and laughing. Three sets of twin girls — a rare blessing. Ramon was still yearning for a boy, and we had one test tube stored in Las Vegas in a cryogenic freezer, sitting unused while our twins had been born in 1996, 1997, and 1998. I was grateful for our large family and kept telling Ramon, with regards to more children, absolutely not. We did have a neighbor in Lebanon with thirteen daughters, and I feared this quest could go on indefinitely.

He caught me at a weak moment, getting me to say yes. We would try one more time, the last time. Having three embryos remaining, a new surrogate was successfully implanted on St. Patrick's Day 2000. We flew to Las Vegas with all the girls and nannies for the procedure, said a prayer for a healthy son. We would name him Patrick, if we were to be so lucky.

We still didn't have a house in Las Vegas. We stayed at Caesars Palace in a three-bedroom suite. Ramon sold our home in preparation for building a bigger new house. He thought he'd made a great deal, selling our home for a container of paintings. It was a collection of art consisting of one thousand paintings made in China, mostly cheap florals and landscapes. He shipped them to Beirut for me to sell, an unsolicited job on top of raising six daughters. I felt overwhelmed. He also let me know he was living in a two-bedroom apartment and I didn't need to visit. I felt confused, sensing an enormous change in him, disconnecting. He was constantly preoccupied and distant, resuming his premarital habit of smoking four packs a day.

Only two weeks into this state of limbo, we made the most of the hospitality at Caesars Palace, then packed up my girls and nannies and headed back to Beirut. The trips back and forth were a major undertaking. Now I was traveling with three sets of twins under three years of age and four nannies — eleven passports, massive diaper bags, and three double strollers. When my mom was with us, it was a dozen travelers. We took advantage of the two suitcases per person limit. I dressed my girls in matching pink jackets in case one of them strayed. I would have used leashes if not for appearances, it can be terrifying to lose a child at a busy airport.

All of us sat tightly together in the coach section, usually traveling Lufthansa. The girls enjoyed the airport in Frankfurt, spending eight-hour layovers between the McDonald's and the large bathrooms. The long layover gave me time to reflect on all these past visits. Something was going on. Ramon was tight-lipped. When visiting his office, I felt all his employees were avoiding me. Photos lined his walls of me and the children, advertising he was a devoted family man. To the outside world Ramon was a loving husband and father, yet he was absent in every imaginable way. During this trip, not once did he pick up his kids to hug and kiss. When in our presence he made sure we were taken care of at the hotel then zoomed back to a life he was keeping a secret. I no longer knew the man I married. Stranger.

We waited five months for the wonderful news that we were going to have a boy. Patrick would be born in December. Our prayers, answered. Ramon was over the moon, feeling this would finally make him happy. Our family would be complete. I dreamed of a brother for my girls where he would always have their back. Perhaps this would be a positive turning point and Ramon would come rushing back to Lebanon, grateful for everything we had accomplished in our ten years together. Was a happy marriage around the corner?

Patrick was born December 3, 2000. We traveled back to Vegas for Patrick's birth and to spend Christmas with Ramon. Christmas also happened to be my birthday, so lots to celebrate. I can't remember which hotel we stayed at, but we still didn't have a house. We ate turkey dinner in a casino restaurant and enjoyed ice cream in one of the poolside cabanas.

With seven kids, four nannies, and my mom, I returned to Beirut with thirty-five pieces of luggage. I was so happy to be home. Lebanon.

The new year was spent trying to figure out what to do with all these paintings Ramon traded for our house in Vegas. Jack and the beanstalk. We still had the large warehouse where Madam President Mona Haraoui would stop by looking for objects to sell at her Chronic Care Center. I had all the paintings unloaded to assess if they had any value. Unexpectedly, some of them were fabulous well-done reproductions with heavy gilt frames. Others were original Dali and Chagall lithographs. I kept an assortment for the palace to cover one of the salon ceilings in renaissance art. I loved the Rembrandt copies. When everything was sorted, I called my friends who owned antique and furniture shops, selling the whole lot at good prices. When the accounting was over, we sold the paintings for half the value of our home in Las Vegas. At least it wasn't a total loss.

And now to arrange a baptism for Patrick. He was an Abi-Rached son, born to carry on the name and bring pride to his family and village. The little prince. Ramon's birthday was August 25, which seemed like an appropriate date for a major celebration. I would invite the president and his wife, politicians, Lebanese businessmen, and our large extended family. Ramon invited his clients and business partners from Las Vegas. Three hundred guests would attend.

In mid-August Ramon jetted into Beirut using the Gulfstream IV on a fourteen-hour flight from Vegas. A few of his clients accompanied him to celebrate Patrick's baptism. We met him on the tarmac along with his two brothers, and I knew he was so proud to finally have a son. Pulling me aside and reaching into his shirt pocket, he handed me a small box. Did he really miss me? I opened the box to a twenty-one-carat white diamond.

"This is for Patrick, thank you."

It was so spectacular and unexpected. Just a few months ago, he acted like I was a stranger. Now he was gifting me with an extravagant symbol of love. At the same time, I was wondering where all this money was coming from and why he was still living in a two-bedroom apartment on the Strip.

Ramon invited several VIP guests from Caesar's Palace along with the vice presidents of Versace Fragrances and Brioni menswear. They would be staying with us at the palace. My sisters arrived from Seattle, Mom was there, and the little chapel was again filled with flowers. I wore a pink suit while Patrick played with my rows and rows of huge white pearls. Only the immediate family had been invited for the afternoon ceremony to witness Patrick's baptism. The rest of the guests were waiting for the big party that evening.

At dusk the guests started arriving in Ferraris, Porsches, and chauffeur-driven limousines — royalty from the nearby Gulf, and the president along with his entire family. It was a black-tie event so the ladies were dressed in lavish garden-colored chiffon and matching jewels. Even the Sheiks wore jewels on their lapels. We dined on fresh lobster cascading down an ice sculpture and caviar by the pound, danced around the pool to a live American jazz band. Of course, there were cases of champagne.

A separate party was going on at the gate for the chauffeurs. They feasted on American style BBQ chicken, steak, and local Lebanese treats. Everyone enjoyed one hour of fireworks. Slowly the partygoers departed one by one, until the sun came up.

The guests from Las Vegas were awestruck, never imagining Beirut to be such an exciting city. For insurance purposes the jet had to get out of Lebanon and return to Las Vegas. We accompanied our American guests to the airport, waving goodbye to them as the Gulfstream lifted off. Ramon planned to stay two more weeks with us, having business with several politicians that could only be handled in person. All were at the baptism shaking hands as family friends, at the same time planning meetings.

One lady in particular was a US Counselor working in the visa department. Ramon lavished her with gifts for a little help with his political friends. She took full advantage of his generosity and helped him to obtain visas for Lebanese citizens hoping to get to the United States. This somehow evolved to where he was handing her twenty passports at a time from people he did not know. The US Embassy was granting visas on Ramon's word alone. It was all about ego and power. Ramon had the cash to make it happen. I watched this escapade with disgust, similar to the Bob Dole illegal campaign contributions, knowing someday it would come back to haunt him.

On September 11, 2001, I took Ramon to the Beirut Airport where he boarded Air France for Paris. He had a connecting flight to New York, and called me between flights in Paris before boarding an Air France flight. Two hours later, my sister called me to turn on CNN. The twin towers were under attack. Ramon was in the air when the plane turned around with no announcement from the flight crew. Finally landing at Charles de Gaulle, he learned about the attack. All flights to the US were canceled. Ramon booked a flight back to Beirut and we watched the aftermath of 9/11 from his office in Bejdarfel.

Ramon spent another two weeks in Lebanon, wheeling and dealing with the local politicians. Our home was full of gun-toting bodyguards and visiting military. We had thirty people for dinner every night, all conversing in Arabic, all men strangers. I didn't know it then, but this was the turning point in our marriage. He didn't want me to know of his whereabouts nor whom he was dealing with. The shroud of secrecy was everywhere. The veil, impenetrable.

When returning to Las Vegas, everyone with a Middle Eastern background was deemed suspicious. Because Ramon held dual American and Lebanese passports, he was questioned by authorities over his travel back and forth. Empty vans, one of them mine for our seven kids, parked in the Las Vegas warehouses were reported by a suspicious neighbor. Most of his employees were Lebanese, and Arabic was a language of convenience throughout the building. He was also constantly shipping us container after container of goods to Lebanon and sending lots of money for his affairs in Beirut. This was all being investigated.

He was gambling every night and would rarely talk about his business. My trips to Las Vegas became less and less frequent, with no home in Vegas. Ramon sold it for paintings. When entering the United States, customs was now questioning my visits to Lebanon and why I had dual passports. His mood swings were becoming more and more violent, and I hated to subject the kids to his temper. We never knew what we were walking into.

I discovered that sometime in 2002 his associate at the US Embassy in Beirut was fired for her assistance to Ramon. It was totally illegal for her to approve visas without an interview. No favors should be granted. One of the passports Ramon passed to her was for a man named Ziad Samir Jarrah, helping this man to obtain a visa to the United States. He was a Lebanese born member of Al-Qaeda who studied in Hamburg with Mohamed Atta. He was living in Florida and enrolled in flight school.

On the morning of 9/11, Ziad piloted the United Airlines Flight 93, crashing into Shanksville, Pennsylvania, and killing all aboard. The plane's intended destination was the US Capitol.

Who on earth was Ramon? What had I missed?

Better question: Was I complicit?

Chapter Eighteen

My World Was Changing

L ebanon was now going through a reconstruction period. Beirut was booming. Money was pouring in from neighboring countries and the price of land was skyrocketing. New construction was everywhere, and the region seemingly at peace. Perhaps returning to its former glory. I tried to convince myself I was living in the right place at the right time, while deep down fearing I've made a huge mistake by moving to this country. A democratic election voted General Emil Lahoud the new president, and Rafik Hariri as the new prime minister. Hariri's downtown development company, Solidere, was bulldozing all the war-torn buildings and creating a major metropolis.

In a few short years, I witnessed the bombed-out buildings giving rise to hotels and skyscrapers. It was all new and beautiful yet remaining with a charm and culture of the Middle East.

Ramon returned to Beirut for Christmas in 2002, staying for a few months. We briefly had a discussion about his involvement in procuring visas through the US Embassy and of course he denied it, telling me I had the wrong information. He knew, I knew, we both knew. Self-deceit.

Ramon returned on a leased jet in mid-February, picking us up along with my girlfriend Marianne and her husband, Henri. We flew to Paris, where Marianne and Henri stayed at their apartment and we stayed at the Hotel de Crillon. It was four days of sightseeing, shopping, and dining. Looking back, it was the last time Ramon and I tried to be a couple. Having fun. No talk of his business or family problems. We were in Paris wanting to escape the outside world. We returned to Lebanon; Ramon flew back to Vegas. We planned to meet again in Paris in mid-July.

All of my six girls were now in school. The spring weather was beautiful. I accompanied my drivers to pick them up about a thirty-minute drive south of our home. Sometimes we would stop at the beach for an impromptu picnic at Eddie Sands in Byblos, a beautiful white-sand resort owned by my friend Alice. Other times we grabbed lunch at a water's edge cafe situated on the rocks in the ancient city of Batroun. Chez Maggie served freshly caught little fish called Sultan Brahim along with tabbouleh and crispy French fries. The kids loved it.

The nannies were always with us, whether eating, playing, or working. They were truly part of the family. My girls were included in the nannies' daily chores: cooking, cleaning, and taking care of all the dogs. The village knew how much we loved animals. Sometimes we found a stray tied to our gates or dropped off at the guardhouse. I'd have it checked out by a vet who'd give it a rabies vaccine. After a month, the dog would be sold to the families in the village for twenty-five dollars. If I didn't put a price on the animal, it would be used for target practice.

On weekends we drove to other villages to watch the monks' pressing olives in their huge stone barrels. Sometimes we drove to visit the duck farms nearby, where foie gras was produced. We were an anomaly in the region. An American family, welcomed wherever we went. Every time we returned to the palace and through the gates, I pinched myself.

Ramon scheduled meetings in Paris with several perfume companies, planning to meet me on July 15, 2003. I could hardly wait to go back to Paris. Ramon was traveling non-stop on Air France from LAX in a few hours. I was on my way to the airport in Beirut when my phone rang.

"Honey I've been arrested." That was all Ramon could say, instructing me not to go to Paris.

In that moment, everything changed. Or, maybe, nothing changed. Maybe, I was just starting to believe what I already knew. My heart sank. Ramon had never been who he said he was. His shady dealings were finally catching up with him, catching up with all of us.

I returned home and unpacked. I was unsure of what Ramon had done to get arrested. It could be more illegal campaign contributions, illegal visa applications, illegal product diversion, or maybe something more sinister like a 9/11 connection. I had to wait forty-eight hours before Ramon finally called.

He'd been arrested for failing to declare sixty thousand dollars in cash he was carrying while boarding the Air France flight to Paris. He'd failed to tell me that he wrapped the money in plastic to smuggle it through customs. Failed to tell me both his passports had been confiscated and he was not allowed to travel. What he did tell me was that he was hiring Robert Shapiro to represent him. Hiring a high-profile attorney for smuggling cash? It didn't add up. Nothing ever added up with Ramon.

The kids were out of school, so I packed up seven children, four nannies, myself, and twenty suitcases to Las Vegas. I needed to talk to my husband and find out what was really going on. Ramon put us up at Caesar's Palace in a four-bedroom suite. We rarely saw him. He was constantly gambling. He couldn't spend time with seven kids when he needed to be at the blackjack table. We stayed a week then flew up to Seattle to visit my family and friends. I needed some stability, needed family, needed to confide.

Margie had been my BFF since the seventies: the days of John Robert Powers Modeling School and our visits to see Howard Shultz at his Starbucks coffee shop; working together teaching girls how to apply make-up and walk down the runway; spending countless evenings together talking about dreams, marriages, men, children, while sipping vodka and listening to Patsy Cline.

It was now thirty years later, and we were still best friends. I shared with her how happy I was with my seven children, but that my husband was never around. That I sensed how dangerous he was, and I had to think of a way to give my girls a normal life. I was becoming afraid of my life in Beirut, and afraid of my husband. If I threatened divorce, he would take my kids away.

Lebanon did not have laws protecting women. I had a Lebanese and a US passport, as did my children. Dual citizenship. With two nationalities in Lebanon, I could open my own bank account and own real estate, but only a Lebanese father could open bank accounts for their children. Only the Lebanese father can apply for passports, and only a Lebanese father can represent his children in legal matters. So, if I chose to give my children money or land, only the father can accept it for them, or give it back to himself. It was definitely a man's world, no rights for a woman.

A Lebanese man has the legal right to divorce his wife, take the kids, and give her no money. I was married in the United States as an American, to a US citizen, so I assumed my rights would be protected and property shared as community property. I told Margie I was afraid to divorce, but was extremely unhappy. I knew Ramon had girlfriends, and our living in two separate continents was not helping the matter.

Ramon was arrested for a serious charge and he was being represented by Robert Shapiro. He was living in a world of litigation, lawyers for his business, his taxes, and his criminal activities. If I threatened divorce, I was not in a position of power. Litigation was not my world. I knew I needed to build a business, to try to earn some money, so I could defend myself and not lose my kids. It was a terrifying thought for a mother, having seven kids, no job, and living in a Middle Eastern country with no rights. Just one year earlier, I thought my life was great. Now, I was looking through the lens of reality, seeing the truth. Trouble was looming.

Upon my return to Beirut, I made up my mind to open a boutique, to do something to make enough money to stash for a future divorce. Several years earlier, I took my children to the Intercontinental Hotel located high in the mountains above Beirut. At six thousand feet above sea level was a fabulous resort called Faraya, surrounded by luxury ski chalets, restaurants, and first-class skiing. Our home was far away from society, so we would spend weekends at the resort with all our friends from the city, skiing, taking walks with the dogs, and eating at fun restaurants. The kids loved meeting up with their friends, seeing a movie, or going bowling. Family fun.

Personally, I was not a good skier, but I loved life at the hotel lodge, sitting outside on the large terrace and watching my kids swoop down the slopes. I like champagne and cappuccino and keeping warm in my fur coats. Sitting in the sun at the edge of the slopes, the idea for a high-end ski wear boutique came to mind. I could sell fur coats and spectacular outfits for all my friends and tourists. I needed a business, and this could be workable, with the added bonus of my kids seeing their mother running a business, rather than only talking and drinking champagne.

I set up a meeting with the manager of the Intercontinental Hotel in Faraya, finding a space for a shop. I immediately called my girlfriend Rim, and she introduced me to the agents at Escada. If I timed this perfectly, I could travel to Munich, Germany, choose some high-end ski wear, and hopefully open prior to January 2005. For me, the epitome of luxury is to wear soft warm fur. A fox and a cow both have skins, and I have always been a proponent of kind treatment to animals. I also prefer to wear fur rather than leather in cold weather, it's just warmer.

I called my friend George Bassil, a very talented interior designer, and in no time, we finalized plans for the boutique. I traveled to Munich and bought the winter ski resort line from Escada. Ramon helped me secure a contract for fur coats. He was on board and enthusiastic that I wanted to work. He had not visited Lebanon since his arrest a year earlier. I was hoping this coming Christmas he would visit the children. Lebanon was really booming, and I was hoping this coming season would bring lots of tourists to my new boutique. It only snowed December through March at this resort, but the season lasted until the snow melts. In April, one can ski in the morning on the slopes, then drive forty-five minutes down the mountains and swim in the Mediterranean Sea. All my friends were so excited for me and promised to be good customers.

Debra Boutique opened early November with no snow outside. It would be another few weeks before the tourists arrived. Coats, jackets, gloves, hats, all fun, filled the boutique. The resort previously only sold rugged ski wear, so I was filling a niche with more glamorous items. Soon the slopes were packed with snow and the tourists arrived in droves. I had mink, fox, chinchilla, and sable. There were fur hats, boas, short jackets, and fur-lined boots. Embroidered ski wear from Escada, fabulous jackets and cashmere sweaters. I even carried lingerie.

Ramon was able to visit for ten days during Christmas, as he had gotten his passport back. He didn't spend one day with the kids. He stayed with his two brothers, organizing meetings and trying to turn his real estate holdings into cash. It was all business, always was.

He let me know he sold a major building, and he needed to sign the papers quickly, so he abruptly flew back to Vegas.

It had been two years since Ramon was in Lebanon. There had been no real communication on this trip. I was told to keep my mouth shut when I tried to ask questions. He never looked me straight in the eye. I was tired of guessing what was wrong. At least I opened a boutique and I was hoping for good sales in case I opted for a divorce. I would have some money on hand independent from Ramon. It may have been a long way off, but at least I was on the right track to independence, if necessary.

February 14, 2005. The boutique had been open for two months. It was a sunny day and the slopes were busy — a great recipe for business. I was optimistic.

News was starting to make its way across the country that a car bomb exploded in front of the downtown Phoenicia Intercontinental Hotel, killing Prime Minister Rafik Hariri, his bodyguards, and twenty-one others. He'd left a meeting at Parliament and had been driving in an armored convoy in between the Phoenicia and the St. George Hotel. The explosion left a large hole in the middle of the city, shattering windows a half-mile away. One thousand kilos of TNT. Was it Al Qaeda, Syrian politicians, Israel? As an American, I was terrified of more to come. As an American living in Beirut, this was normal everyday life.

The assassination was frontpage news all over the world, and I watched CNN for days. The tourists canceled their reservations, fearing more bloodshed. Uncertainty.

The bombings escalated violently, with fourteen cars with politicians and bodyguards targeted within a few months. It was a war to change the democratic policies of the existing government and replace those in power. Hezbollah, Al Qaeda, Palestinians, and Israel, all vying for power and security. No one trusted the others. Violence and fear won.

I found myself living in a time bomb, waiting to explode. I needed to sell fur coats in the middle of the desert to have a chance to get out.

Good luck with that.

Chapter Nineteen

Escape to Versailles

The assassination of Rafik Hariri changed everything in Beirut. Prior to his killing, I'd felt a sense of prosperity and progress in the reconstruction of Lebanon. New residential towers had been constructed and a fabulous downtown shopping arcade had been built within the ancient ruins of the Phoenicians. The stones and pillars of ancient civilizations were the backdrop for modern restaurants and luxury boutiques. Tourists flocked to see a modern city rise up on the battleground site of a civil war lasting more than twenty years.

Hariri, a Sunni Muslim allied with Saudi Arabia, had been intent on rebuilding Lebanon. He'd had the support of the majority in government and the backing of very wealthy individuals in the region who saw the potential of a new Beirut, the impact it could have locally and regionally. Lebanon was previously the destination of the global jetsetters and had then been making a comeback, and so had been the price of real estate.

The public reconstruction corporation Hariri formed, Solidere, had envisioned a city both modern and ancient. Half the city had been war-ravaged, riddled with bullet holes, and had needed to be torn down. Private landowners had been issued stock in the corporation only to find their buildings bulldozed in the middle of the night to make way for a wider street or a public park. Common owners in a grand city had lost their individual rights to rebuild for a profit. To complicate matters, Hariri, as prime minister, had manipulated the price of the stock to render the value practically worthless. It was theft of a city and its inhabitants on a grand scale. His supporters became his enemies. His assassination, and the assassination of the fourteen other politicians supporting him, was a power grab. The opposition seized the opportunity, retaking power and the billions of dollars at stake.

I had opened my boutique during the height of Hariri's power, when the future of the country was looking its brightest. The rich were spending money in the new restaurants and shops springing up on every corner: Chanel, Gucci, Dior opening their doors to eager customers with black American Express cards. My boutique fit right in. The city may have been smoldering from car bombs, but the women wanted chinchillas. My seven kids were skiing, while I wore my latest and most expensive fur coat to sip my cappuccino. I talked to my fashionable friends, and the coat would sell before noon. I'd go get another coat to wear to cocktail hour and before it was time for dinner, another sale. The furs were flying off my shoulders.

My friends showed their support for my boutique, but secretly I feared Debra Boutique may not withstand the political turmoil. I needed money to pay for a divorce that was inevitable. Luckily, I sold nearly my entire collection, placing an order for more minks and chinchillas. I hoped life in Beirut would be back to normal in a few short months.

What I found fascinating about life in Beirut was the will to survive. Nothing mattered except family, friends, and food. Bombs exploding in the distance? Turn the music up louder to finish the dance. Or hop a plane to anywhere and wait for a ceasefire. We could hardly wait to get back to Beirut, with the unlimited invitations to the Embassy dinners, festivals, and grand galas.

Charity balls were an excuse to show off your wealth and establish your family name as a grand philanthropist. Ramon paid a fee of twenty-five thousand dollars to become a member of the Knights of Malta, an international organization with Catholic roots. It was very charitable, raising money for hospitals and dedicating themselves to easing suffering and sickness worldwide.

The biggest benefactor in Lebanon for this charity was Prince Edward Lobkowitz who married Princess Francoise de Bourbon Parme. She was a descendant of French royalty. They were raising money for a hospital in the mountains above Beirut for handicapped persons and visited Lebanon frequently. I had met them at an evening soiree at Angelique's and subsequently invited them to my home in Bejdarfel. It was thirty people at Chateau St. Antoine for lunch, spending a wonderful afternoon together. We drank a case of Chateau Margaux. For dessert, we ordered small cakes with their coats of arms in frosting. They were clearly touched.

Not long after this lunch, we received an invitation from the Knights of Malta for a charity dinner at the Palace of Versailles. Springtime in Paris. At a one-thousand-dollar donation per plate, I begged Ramon for two tickets. Perhaps it could be an occasion for me to see my husband, as our visits had become less and less frequent. Two days before the dinner, Ramon canceled. Shannon hopped on a plane the next day. I wore Dior black lace and diamonds. Shannon wore platinum silk and rubies. Both of us were draped in fur from my boutique.

I hired a private car to drive us to the Château de Versailles, thinking of Jackie Kennedy Onassis when she dined with President De Gaulle at this same palace. We were escorted through a side entrance to attend a private mass in the Royal Chapel of Louis XIV. After mass, there was a private tour of Versailles, and then we were allowed to wander through the halls, taking pictures in front of the grand object's d'art, paintings, and tapestries. My favorite was the Queen's bedroom, elegant.

Princess Lobkowitz was the guest of honor, along with Madame Chirac, the wife of the current French president. Most of the men were wearing tuxedos and those draped silk ribbons laden with medals only royals are allowed to wear. All the ladies wore brooches of diamonds. Shannon and I took photos with Prince Alexander of Yugoslavia, whom I met in Beirut before.

We were then escorted into the Gallery of Great Battles in the South Wing of the Palace, a room nearly four hundred feet long. Round tables seating ten were decorated with antique candlesticks and bouquets of white lilies. We sat with other guests from Lebanon but were able to mix and mingle with everyone in attendance. The Prince and Princess Lobkowitz greeted all of us warmly while we dined on medallions of veal. I never wanted the evening to end. I was in heaven.

Shannon and I stayed in Paris several more days, discussing my marital situation, hoping for the best for me. I was unable to share with anyone else the depth of my confusion, despair, and heartache. To the outside world I lived like a queen, but I sensed something sinister was brewing in my palace.

How had my life evolved to this duality?

I was living life like a queen, but I felt more like a Mafia princess, always looking over her shoulder. Shannon and I discussed what divorce might look like, fantasizing an amicable parting with shared assets and shared time with the children. Deep down I knew Ramon would take the kids and put me penniless on the street. Or worse, I'd become an inconvenient woman that wouldn't survive a car accident. His pride and his pocketbook couldn't allow for the scandal of divorce.

Summer was coming to an end and I knew I had to go back to Las Vegas. We hadn't seen Ramon for at least six months. I tearfully said goodbye to Shannon and we each hopped on a plane back to reality.

Chapter Twenty
High Life and Low Lives

Patrick was born December of 2000. He was now five years old. At the time of his birth, we purchased a teardown house on Tomiyasu Street in Las Vegas, close to the airport. The kids needed a home in Las Vegas. It was a fabulous two-acre lot. I worked on a two-story design with a grand staircase leading to all the bedrooms upstairs. Ramon was still living between the casinos and a small, rented apartment, while we stayed in hotel suites when visiting. I was delusional to think our marriage could be saved, but I was still hoping for the best.

Ramon mentioned he wanted to surprise me with a new home on the lot purchased so long ago.

Completely unbeknown to me, he had fired the original architect and changed all the plans. Living in Beirut and busy with the kids and my boutique, I'd had no idea he was changing course. We were making small talk daily, but we never had a conversation lasting longer than five minutes. It really didn't matter if we had another grand home. All we needed was a home for seven kids when we visited Vegas. Ramon let me know he'd been working on it for the past two years and the costs were staggering. I was looking forward to this surprise. A real place to stay on our visits might improve our relationship.

Summer arrived, so I packed up the kids and the nannies and booked our flights to Las Vegas. We would finally have a house and wouldn't be staying in any more casino suites. To my surprise the original house was never demolished. He simply remodeled the old one with cheap floor tiles and not enough bedrooms. It still had low ceilings, tiny bathrooms, and no playroom for our seven children. The nannies squeezed into a bedroom with Patrick. The laundry room was in a corner in the garage. Most of all I hated the uncomfortable sofas covered in embroidered fabrics and cheap garish paintings decorating the house. It looked like a fast-food restaurant on the side of the freeway.

At least Ramon was out of his tiny apartment and we had a real estate asset in Las Vegas. A fortune had been wasted on a cheap remodel and I was not allowed to ask questions. A constant flow of low-life visitors arriving and departing. Meetings were held behind closed doors. Ramon's employees were polite, but remained closed-mouthed and secretive. The kids were startled when Ramon screamed at them for no reason at all, then turned his anger at me. We were afraid and tried not to be around.

Laying on Ramon's desk was a copy of a newly published book, *Whale Hunt in the Desert* by Deke Castleman. It was an expose revealing secrets in Las Vegas authored by a casino host named Steve Cyr. Ramon had an entire chapter written about him. My husband, the book claimed, established a half-million-dollar line of credit at each of fifty-six casinos around the world. At Atlantis in the Bahamas, a credit line of one million dollars. I didn't know he even went to the Bahamas. The book claimed he had his own Boeing 727 which he used to fly into his Palace in Lebanon with eighty-six rooms and ninety attendants. There were photos of the jets and so many smiling Lolita's. I was disgusted. It further stated he had so much money that all his losses at gambling did not even make a dent. Who was this man that I am married to, and why was he spinning a web of lies about everything in our life?

We only stayed a month. Before our departure, we spent a week at Walmart preparing our thirty suitcases for the return trip. I needed boy clothes for Patrick and clothes for the girls who were starting school. I was stashing fur coats between the kids' play clothes to add to the inventory at my boutique. My mom was traveling back with us and visited for several months. She loved spending time with her grandkids and I needed her love and support.

My life in Lebanon was a fairytale. My children and I lived in a castle filled with love and freedom. I had wonderful friends and a social life full of lunches at the beach resorts and glamorous parties at private mansions. I could play with my kids and enjoy weekend retreats at our mountain chalet. I was gaining a reputation with my boutique where everyone wanted to shop. I was blessed with an amazing life in Lebanon because my husband lived on the other side of the planet.

We had everything we needed, allowing me to look the other way and ignore his girlfriends, his shady business partners, and his lack of respect for money. I was taken care of as long as I asked no questions and kept my mouth shut. This wasn't an honest life or marriage. I was setting an example for my children of what a relationship was and I felt ashamed. I want to raise my children to be proud of me. How could I by living in a sham marriage and allowing my husband to treat me and my kids as commodities. Pawns in his game of chess. Expendable.

Were there any solutions to get me and my children away from this farce? Was I destined to wait it out until I was old and they were all married?

I was not looking forward to spending another twenty years in my gilded cage.

Spring vacation was approaching, and I booked a mini vacation to Sharm el Sheik, Egypt. Whenever we traveled, it was always back and forth to Las Vegas. The kids never experienced any other place in the world. We took an eighty-minute flight to Egypt, spending four days swimming in hotel pools and snorkeling in the clear waters of the Red Sea. At night, we went to outdoor cafes to watch the swirling Moroccan dancers, spinning for hours in white tunics to the sounds of Oriental music. The food was wonderful: chicken, fried fish, potatoes, and tabouli. It was a great time.

During our last lunch, loudspeakers announced, "Please return to your hotels." Our flights home were in the evening. When we reached the airport, a sense of danger permeated the entire airport. I feared we may be detained, and the plane would not take off, leaving us stranded in Egypt. Our passports were stamped, and we were steered into an area waiting to board. A lot of commotion was going on, with everyone yelling in Arabic. We were finally ushered onto the plane and sat for two more hours on the ground. At last, we were given clearance to depart and took off for Beirut.

That evening it was announced there had been a terrorist attack not far from our hotel and all planes had been grounded. Our flight was the last to depart. It seemed like everywhere I turned the Middle East was about to explode. It was still several years before the Arab Spring, where anti-government protests would rock the entire region, but you could feel the tension mounting. No one was happy with their leaders.

Upon returning from Egypt, I received an invitation to the Cannes Film Festival in the south of France. One of my friends was doing public relations for Fawaz Gruosi, the owner of de Grisogono Jewels. She invited me as her guest to attend several VIP events. Fawaz had married Caroline Schuefele, the heiress of the Chopard family of watches and jewelry. Caroline worked with celebrities at the Cannes Film Festival and most red-carpet events, including the Academy Awards in Hollywood, dressing them in gowns and jewels before walking the red carpet.

My friend was staying at the Hotel Majestic, just across the street from the red-carpet ceremonies, and the location where Caroline dressed her celebrity clients. I was two hotels down at the Hotel Martinez. At breakfast, I sat next to Harvey Weinstein, the movie producer, who was accompanied by his wife Georgina Chapman. She was absolutely beautiful, there to dress her celebrity clients in ball gowns from her Marchesa brand. Harvey looked overweight and unshaven. We were there for a party given by de Grisogono, to be held at Eden Roc Hotel. I wore a burgundy silk dress by George Chakra with a plunging neckline to show off my rubies. It normally was a ten-minute drive from my hotel to the Eden Roc, but I waited two hours for the car. I guess they forgot to put my name on the celebrity limo list.

It was an amazing event. Top models were dressed in huge pieces of de Grisogrono jewelry. Paris Hilton danced with Tommy Hilfiger. I sat at a long rectangular table, next to Diane Von Furstenberg and everyone was a celebrity. There were long dresses, short dresses, tuxedos and jeans. Live music played all night on the outdoor terrace overlooking the Mediterranean. Hundreds of yachts were moored in the Bay of Cannes. Paris never stopped dancing, nor did Ivana Trump. I drank my champagne and table hopped all night.

I met a very glamorous woman, very outspoken and fun, who invited me to a party the following night. We rendezvoused at the marina in Cannes for a private yacht party given by the jeweler Van Cleef and Arpels. Roberto Cavalli's yacht was docked next to where I was invited, and you could see him and models drinking and dancing. Paparazzi were everywhere, snapping photos and taking notes. I ending up spending most of the evening with Stanilas De Querize, the new CEO of Van Cleef. He was charming and handsome, and we spoke of Beirut and Paris and the days of the 1960s when glamor was at its height. He gave me his card if I ever was in Paris.

Returning to Beirut three days later, I looked forward to seeing my mom again who was still at the Palace with the nannies and kids. She lived her life through my adventures and I could hardly wait to tell her about the South of France. She wanted to hear about all the celebrities and what they were wearing.

Business had been great these past two years, and I was considering opening a second shop in the downtown area of Beirut. The Phoenicia had an empty storefront close to the lobby. I was making a profit in my mountain resort boutique, but I needed to stash a few hundred thousand dollars to make leaving Ramon possible. Another fur boutique should provide twice the profits. Banking in Beirut was private and secure, allowing me and Ramon to establish separate personal accounts. I didn't know what was in his bank and he didn't know what was in mine.

I took the plunge and signed the lease on a second boutique. It was my only way out. Opening my boutiques gave me an identity. My bank account was growing and perhaps someday I could see the light at the end of a very long tunnel. I was selling fur coats in the Middle East, praying for snow in the desert.

Chapter Twenty-One
War and Refugees

The new year brought even more political turmoil to the Middle East. President George Bush declared he wanted to eliminate Hezbollah and was going to authorize strikes if Israel was hit by any kind of attack. Israel and Lebanon technically had been at war since 1967, and you could feel the tensions escalating. The border zone between the two countries was heavily armed and any misfired weapon could provoke an international incident.

All tickets were purchased in order to bring the children to Las Vegas for their summer vacation. We were planning on staying a month. I would be traveling with my mom and only three nannies. My children were now six to ten years old.

A week prior to our departure, Israel attacked the strongholds of Hezbollah. Lebanon was now at war. I was an American citizen living in a remote village high in the hills in northern Lebanon, far away from the southern border with Israel. The airports closed and the population was in a panic. My travel plans needed an update.

Many of my friends left prior to the attack, sensing the escalation. Lebanon had always been on the brink of war, and I concluded one more week wouldn't change anything. Other friends were applying for refugee status and waiting to be evacuated. My friend Mary, left for Ireland, traveling to Syria by car and then flying out of Damascus. Marianne left by helicopter and then transferred to a plane for France. I had seven kids, three nannies, and my mother all needing to be evacuated.

We decided to wait to see if this would just blow over, believing President Bush would not allow a full-out annihilation of the country. I expected it to be over in a few weeks with Israel defeating Hezbollah. What the world did not know was just how strong Hezbollah was, and their stockpile of weapons. Hezbollah was holding ground with their backing from Iran. With every Israeli attack, they fought back using long range missiles. Israel was now sending fighter jets to Tripoli to my north and Baalbek to my east. The flight path to Baalbek was directly over my house. Jets passed so close to the roof of my house, I could see the pilot and read the call numbers on the plane. We were surrounded by war.

At night the jets were flying with no lights, you could only hear the engines and the sound of bombs exploding in the distance. My mom remembered the blackouts of World War II, and wanted me to close all my curtains and turn off the lights, she was so afraid. I figured I was not a target, as they wanted to strike the cities, troops, bridges, phone towers, and oil refinery tanks. The refinery bombings created an environmental hazard that blackened all the beaches on the coast. I never left my home, unless to buy food. My closest friends all left. The cell tower close to my home was destroyed, so now there was no phone service to communicate with Ramon.

Our village was so remote, it made me feel safe. We were even having picnics on the grass to pass the time. One morning Mary's husband, Roderick, arrived at my gate with his housekeeper, who was friends with my nannies. It had been two weeks of bombing, and he needed to take a break and get out of the city. All the cell towers were destroyed, but he knew I was still in the country and would be at home.

We were all together having lunch in the garden when a huge explosion rocked the village. This was different; it was close to our home. Roderick left after lunch, and I told my kids it was time for us to leave. My kids were old enough to sense real danger was around the corner. I called the US Embassy to inquire about being evacuated. It so happened the last evacuations for US citizens and for those holding visas would take place the next day. We had to be at the evacuation site at six in the morning. It was our only chance to leave. Only one carry-on piece of luggage per person. I took jeans, jewels, and credit cards, not knowing when we would return.

The next morning all twelve of us were at the Port of Beirut for security clearance. My mom was in a wheelchair. My kids were excited and looking forward to the adventure, no fear. All around us people were screaming in Arabic and crying goodbyes, so much chaos and confusion. The other evacuees carried all their belongings in enormous fabric suitcases tied with rope or nylon cords. The US military inspected our papers and passports, and we were cleared to board the bus, which would take us to the waiting boat. We boarded an Italian hydrofoil, all Lebanese refugees, except us. We were the only American evacuees.

The hydrofoil cruised for five hours between Beirut and Cyprus. We passed US Navy destroyers. Helicopter after helicopter flew overhead, picking up refugees to fly to Cyprus and returning back to collect more. I stood outside on deck in the fresh air, because most of the passengers were seasick and the inside of the boat reeked of vomit. Outside on the deck it was so windy we had to hang on while watching the military actions surrounding us. It was as if we were in the middle of a movie.

We arrived at night in Cyprus, passing another check point where an attendant abruptly informed us the nannies could go no further, then started to direct us to the Fairgrounds. It was an open tent with perhaps one thousand temporary beds and SaniCan toilets lining the walls. I argued with the attendant that our papers were in order and we had been cleared. My voice was loud enough to attract the Cyprus officials who confirmed that all of us must leave Cyprus. A US official led us to the waiting plane. I breathed a sigh of relief. I could only imagine me and the kids with my mom in her wheelchair being ushered into the tent of single beds and SaniCan to fend for ourselves.

World Airways is an airline chartered by the US government to bring troops in and refugees out during a crisis. Most refugees on our plane had never flown before, so did not know how to buckle their seatbelts or that smoking was prohibited. So many people were trying to light their cigarettes the flight attendants were desperately trying to maintain control. The crowded plane took off without us being informed of our flight plan or destination. This plane was piloted by the US military and their mission was to get out of the danger zone. One kid next to me tried to open the hatch door at thirty-five thousand feet to see what was on the other side. I assumed we were headed to the United States or possibly a military base in Europe.

We landed at an airbase outside of Philadelphia. Safe. I called Ramon, letting him know we were out of Lebanon and anxious to get to Las Vegas. I was stranded with my entourage and needed his help. His reply: "It is inconvenient for you to come to Vegas and you should go see your sister in Seattle."

No words can describe the feeling of abandonment, disrespect. Numb. I'd called my husband to help us and was dismissed. We were apparently inconvenient.

The airline counters were overwhelmed with the arrival of the World Airways refugee evacuation. Most of my fellow travelers had no final destination, spoke no English, and had no money. I was another refugee who needed assistance, so I was pointed to the end of the line to wait my turn. I called Shannon. She had no hesitation. We were on our way to Seattle. I was so grateful.

When landing at SeaTac airport we were met by a large television crew from KOMO. One of Shannon's best friends was in the media and heard our story. Our evacuation was a big story for the evening news. Microphones were thrust in front of us and cameras filmed our arrival. My six-year-old son, Patrick, described on camera how everyone on the boat was throwing-up and how happy he was to be away from the danger. This war was front page news and we had just evacuated as refugees from the front lines. We had traveled for forty-eight hours on a military evacuation to arrive in the safety of my hometown. Everyone was exhausted. An experience of a lifetime, one I never wanted to repeat.

Chapter Twenty-Two
Whose House Is This

After having been safely evacuated, it was now summer vacation. Kids have a short memory, so we were ready to make the most of the beautiful weather in the Pacific Northwest. We arrived with only carry-on luggage and credit cards. I checked us into the Hilton Hotel in Bellevue and went directly to Macy's. Red Robin was across the street to satisfy the kids, and Shannon lived nearby.

This was my birthplace, and I took the time to show my kids the beauty of the San Juan Islands. We drove to Anacortes, hopping on the ferry to Friday Harbor and went whale watching. We took ferries to Bremerton and visited the Naval Shipyards. We went to the Space Needle for lunch. I wasn't going to let war in the Middle East and an uncaring, thoughtless husband put a damper on our summer.

We stayed a month before heading to Vegas. The new house was outfitted with a high-level security system. A push of a button and all the windows and doors would be closed and secured by metal shutters. It scared me. This was Las Vegas, not Beirut. His home office had a security camera system of twenty closed circuit cameras wired between the house and his office, separated by only a few blocks. The office had the same set-up so Ramon could watch his home, office, employees, and warehouse from wherever he sat. His office had no windows. Now his house, our home, had a lock down button. When the sun went down, I was instructed to push the button and close us all inside. We would keep ourselves occupied with the TV until he left at dusk to gamble every single night. Confinement. Clockwork.

He would leave for three or four hours, returning with a paper shopping bag filled with twenty thousand, fifty thousand or even a hundred thousand dollars in neatly wrapped packages of hundred-dollar bills. All of it went in the safe. A money counter was always on his desk, and he asked me to help him count everything in the safe. I fed all the hundred-dollar bills through the counter, wrapping them in bundles of ten thousand dollars with bank paper currency straps. It totaled seven million dollars. It was stacked in the safe. It was a pile but not as large as one might think. It could have fit into a Samsonite suitcase. It was enough money to change someone's life, to buy homes and cars and put all your kids through college. Instinctively I knew this money was never real. I considered him a professional gambler and he could lose it all by next week. It was, after all, his money.

Several men, who Ramon called investors, were constantly in and out of the house. He told me he was doing a perfume deal or DeSage Chocolates deal, and the investors were all in for part of the profit. Strange roommates. It made me uncomfortable.

Ramon was in business several years back with Ralph Englestad, owner of the Imperial Palace Hotel. Ralph was a constant figure in Ramon's life, a true Las Vegas legend, having made his fortune by selling a piece of land to Howard Hughes for the North Las Vegas Airport.

Ralph was one of Ramon's first investors, lending money for different deals. He trusted Ramon and the two of them would hang out for hours chain smoking at the lobby bar in the Imperial Palace Casino. Ralph trained himself to sleep between four o'clock and eight o'clock twice daily, so he would have time to work and time to drink, always separate shifts. Ramon was a heavy smoker, normally lighting up four packs a day, and Ralph was close behind. Ralph always offered the use of his private aircraft along with his private pilot.

Ralph died in 2002 and Ramon hired his pilot to work as a private secretary and personal assistant for Ramon's business, Cadeau Express. I was seeing a lot of the pilot, helping me with show tickets or arranging a weekend trip to Disneyland to get us out of Ramon's hair.

Ramon was anxious like never before. The investors were constantly at the house having serious meetings and now attorneys were there as well. Ramon shared a little information to quell my curiosity, letting me know he borrowed thirty million dollars from Ralph before he died. Ralph's widow, Betty, discovered the unpaid debt and was now suing Ramon and his entities. My husband thought he was going to lose thirty million dollars. The only thought running through my mind was the thirty million he borrowed. Where was it? We surely had no assets to show for that kind of wealth. Could he be hiding it somewhere, or have invested it in some get rich quick scam? Were there other investors with similar lawsuits? I had so many unanswered questions. Ramon simply told me it was none of my fucking business.

Ramon left the house one day with his attorney, looking like they were heading to the guillotine. When returning hours later, they were jubilant. Somehow Ramon won the case and only had to pay back three million dollars. How could he borrow thirty million dollars and only have to pay back three million dollars because Ralph died? It seemed like an illegal gain to me, and I wondered how the IRS would see it.

Even though war was raging in Beirut, I could hardly wait to get out of Vegas and back home. I hated Vegas. The temperature climbed to one hundred twenty-seven degrees in the afternoon, making playtime outdoors impossible. We had no friends or family in Las Vegas. Ramon created a social life around his investors and he kept busy with them. When the sun went down, we could swim in the pool or head over to the bowling alley at the Green Valley Ranch Casino, were there were fifty bowling lanes and it was child friendly. My girls all wanted me to be on their team because I didn't roll gutter balls.

Not knowing when the fighting would be over, I enrolled the children in school in Las Vegas. Neither French nor Arabic was offered, and since the kids were now speaking three languages, they felt completely out of sorts. Attending schools in Lebanon had given them an advantage in math and science, but they were behind in US history and team sports. On comparing schools, Beirut offered a huge advantage. All my children were now attending school and I was hoping they would make some friends. It would be fun for the kids to play with other kids outside our family. But Ramon rejected the idea of any of us forming relationships or allowing anyone to peek into our private lifestyle. I really wanted to get out of Las Vegas and go home.

Ramon, as usual, was rarely home and one day asked me to drop the kids off at his office so he could show them his warehouse. I was driving our large twelve-passenger van, so after picking up groceries I stopped in to get the children. Walking through the offices toward the back rooms, I was overcome by an intense smell of paint remover. I opened the back door to the warehouse, and all my children were lined up at a table, stripping expiration dates off of bottled water. No masks, no ventilation. Cleaning up case after case to be reprinted and resold. I was looking at my kids working in an illegal sweatshop and ready to pass out.

The minute a cease-fire was announced, we were on a plane heading back to Beirut.

Chapter Twenty-Three
Whatever Happens in Vegas

It was amazing how quickly life was returning to normal in Lebanon after such a horrific summer. The bombing left most of the bridges demolished, cutting off our routes to the children's schools. The detour took nearly two hours each way. The cell towers were repaired, so at least we had telephones for communication. The sad thing was the devastation of the beaches. Now they were covered with gobs of tar from the bombed oil tanks. Foreign embassies offered to clean stretches of the beach. Volunteers spent months removing the unrefined oil. Small amounts appeared for years to come, ruining my kids' bathing suits and making all the local fish inedible. It was an ecological disaster.

The country was again at peace. Hezbollah stepped in with money from Iran to help the refugees, offering money to rebuild homes and shops that had been annihilated from the bombings, giving out money so people could eat. More generous and more organized than our local government, they gained a lot of popularity. The support Bush gave Israel to bomb our southern border and wipe out Hezbollah backfired. Hezbollah was now stronger than ever.

My life in Beirut was full of children's activities, girlfriends, living in a dream palace. My two boutiques kept me busy and winter season was around the corner. The new location in downtown Beirut was gorgeous. I was starting to produce charity fashion shows within the hotel—lady lunches, top models, minks and chinchillas. My children were opening and closing the shows wearing brightly colored fox wraps and boas. They liked being a part of mom's business.

My life in Las Vegas was full of confusion and fear of the unknown. I returned with the children for a brief ten-day visit, where Ramon only had time to spend Christmas Eve with us. He was gambling heavily every night while telling me he was broke. Where did the thirty million go? Our fighting was escalating, and he was taking it out on the kids. They all tried so hard to get to know their father, but he didn't have time for any of us.

In desperation he started a new venture with the CEO of Planet Hollywood, Sir Robert Earl. They formed a company to distribute amenities through an office within Planet Hollywood, who in turn redirected all phone calls back to Cadeau Express. It was a front. They hired a pretty pole dancer named Tara to greet customers. Her outfits consisted of Herve Leger band-aid dresses and Christian Louboutin shoes. I didn't ask questions.

I still had no idea what Ramon's real business was. He sold DeSage Chocolates at Neiman Marcus. Taxi cabs were plastered with ads of seductive models fondling the gold wrapped candy. He had a warehouse filled with shampoo and bottles of water, but nowhere could I find the inventory of costly perfume, crystal, or China he used to sell. The investors were always hanging around listening to Ramon tell them how much money they were all making. There was constantly the talk of millions of dollars in profits, all on the manipulation of the proforma invoices. Money was streaming in and streaming out, it all seemed just too tempting and they all wanted to jump in on the bandwagon.

In a town like Vegas, some of it was bound to get lost on the tables. Perhaps Ramon thought he could just roll the dice and keep the game going, double or nothing. Don't let anyone call your bluff. Not wanting to be around any of it, I preferred the jetlag and ten-hour time change to evenings in Las Vegas wondering how much money Ramon was losing a night.

Only in Las Vegas for a short time, I noticed the secretary he hired to work at the Planet Hollywood Casino was also working at the office of Cadeau Express. Her son was the same age as Patrick and

Ramon was promoting for us to be friends. We had lunch together a few times, but something was fishy. She was just too friendly with Ramon. Her skirts were too tight and she could flip her hair really well.

Did I know Ramon had girlfriends? Of course. Several of my friends visited Ramon in Las Vegas, returning to Beirut to let me know my husband was always accompanied by an escort. I didn't want to believe them. I was fabulous and we had seven children together. I always stood up for him and looked the other way when something negative was said. I couldn't imagine he would cheat on me. He had business problems but we were still married. But a woman knows. I knew. Self-deceit.

My friends described the energy of the penthouse suites Ramon kept at Planet Hollywood and the Wynn Hotel as a bachelor pad. My friends were invited upstairs after a night of gambling or after taking them to a gentlemen's club on Paradise Road for intimate table dancing. He was always holding the arm of a gorgeous blond or brunette and surely it wasn't me.

I felt betrayed. Wife of fifteen years. Seven amazing children. Were we only here to give him credibility? Were we only photos on the wall?

I kept my mouth shut. I still couldn't afford a divorce and was afraid he would take the kids. I couldn't let the D word slip out in anger. My two boutiques were doing well, but I still needed a couple years to fill my bank accounts for lawyers.

His business may have been all smoke and mirrors, but at his disposal was an army of attorneys that would fight me to the end of time.

I guess for now, whatever happened in Vegas, needed to stay in Vegas.

Chapter Twenty-Four
We'll Always Have Paris

I expanded my business with a larger shop in the ski resort and a second shop at the Phoenicia Hotel in downtown Beirut. My jeweler friend, Harry, owned a fabulous shop in the hotel. He told me stories about the eighth-floor hotel guests who have money to burn. These guests were from the nearby Middle East countries, escaping their rigid laws to explore all the pleasures a man could imagine in Beirut. Alcohol and Russian women were at the top of the list.

In the hotel boutique I paid special attention to the black American Express cards on file with instructions: chinchilla for the wives and rabbit for the girlfriends. Imagine an elegant gentleman entering the boutique with his well-dressed wife. Allowing her to choose whatever she wanted. Trying on high-end sables and chinchilla, showering her husband in kisses. As soon as she departed the store, he would be whispering in my ear, "send me a dozen rabbits to my suite on the eighth floor." I knew its real meaning. He was entertaining those gorgeous Russian girls. I was always discreet. Selling a lot of rabbits. A lot!

I was expanding my inventory, carrying those fabulous jeweled handbags by Judith Leiber. Each one sold between one thousand and five thousand dollars in 2007. I had a wonderful personal collection of about twenty bags. Each one had unique shapes like pandas, asparagus, and swans. It had been the chic item at the moment. Ladies piling their bags in the middle of the table at a Michelin-starred restaurant to compare the latest designs.

I teamed up with Harry, producing fashion shows during the ski season in Faraya. The Hotel Intercontinental built a fifty-foot runway outdoors at the foot of the slopes. Top models from Russia strutted down the catwalk wearing furs from Debra Boutique, Jewels from Harry Khatchwajian, and bikinis from Alice's Edde Sands Resort. Business was amazing.

I found myself busy between my two boutiques as tourists were returning and the ski resort was booming. The war and our evacuation were only a short time ago, yet a sense of calm was returning to Lebanon. I was living the good life again, partying, dining, shopping, and fashion. I was in the middle of it all, with photos of my fashion shows in all the magazines. The boutiques gave me a bit of fame and notoriety. There were requests for television interviews and magazine spreads supporting my efforts. As an American girl in Beirut, I was becoming a version of Lawrence of Arabia. Along with my seven children and my love for Lebanon, there was always an angle to write about to feed the masses. A perfect storm I was riding to freedom.

My girlfriends organized a week-long trip to France for Paris Fashion Week. It was only a four-hour flight from Beirut, and all the Lebanese designers would give us front row seats. Elie Saab, George Chakra, Zuhair Murad, and Reem Akra were all becoming big players on the world stage. Rabia Keyrouz was my close friend, living only five minutes from my home in Bejdarfel. He and I shared many lunches and afternoon teas together, talking about food and fashion while overlooking the beaches of the Mediterranean from the port of Batroun. Rabia invited us to see his collection from his atelier in Paris.

We shopped on Avenue Montaigne at Dior and Chanel, then had lunch at L'Avenue just to watch the celebrities. We were lucky, snagging seats to Valentino and Christian LaCroix shows. These were major events with top models, singers, and VIPs. And, of course, we wore our furs from Debra Boutique.

My confidence was soaring, so I called Stanilas De Querize, the CEO of Van Cleef. Always a gentleman, he invited me to an event at his newly opened flagship store on the Place Vendome, just across from the Ritz. When arriving, I was greeted personally by Stanlias and escorted to a private back room behind the main boutique. In our last conversation we'd spoken about the glamor of the 1960s and the magnificent jewels of that time. He wanted to show me the private collection where all these priceless gems were on display. Case after case of unimaginable beauty and superb craftsmanship—I was awestruck.

After the tour we returned to the main boutique, and I recognized Mohammed Al Fayed, owner of the Ritz Hotel. He was the father of Dodi El Fayed, the boyfriend of Princess Diana, who tragically died with her in that car crash. The three of us drank champagne, then Mohammed walked across the plaza, back toward the Ritz. I could hardly wait to tell all my girlfriends about my night out.

We returned from the City of Lights to a chaotic political situation in Beirut. The husband of my best friend Marianne was now on the list of political targets. For safety he moved into the residential wing of the Phoenicia Hotel, guarded by high security. The entire wing had been taken over to protect these very important targeted individuals. Marianne would stop by my boutique and we would go up together to see Henri. It was so stressful for her family. They were worried for his safety. Living in Lebanon meant trying to balance the fear of a third-world dangerous country with the joy of seeking happiness.

I was always amazed at how quickly Beirut jumped back to life when there was such a continual sense of danger. I was selling fur coats in the lobby of the Intercontinental Hotel while my best girlfriend's husband was sequestered upstairs in the same hotel for fear of assassination. We would be dining at the best restaurants and drinking champagne when a car bomb nearby exploded killing the most revered diplomat or a high-ranking politician. Paradox.

My life was evolving. I loved Beirut, my children, my friends, and my fabulous home. I was at the top of my game, invited everywhere and photographed for all the magazines. My fur boutiques were doing well and I had an opportunity to expand into Dubai where they were building an indoor manmade ski slope. Imagine the volume of chinchilla I could sell there to all the princesses on their way to St. Moritz. On the outside it was a perfect life, my path golden. On the inside, I was terrified of my husband if I rocked the boat.

Chapter Twenty-Five

Charades

No longer was I questioning it anymore. My role in this marriage was to be his beautiful wife, with fancy jewels, providing him credibility. Having seven kids makes him look grounded and respectable.

Nobody could fathom how uncaring he was. Nobody.

I called him daily, as a loving wife should, trying to nurture a connection. I never knew what mood he would be in. Sometimes he would answer the phone: "Hi, honey, how are you?" Sometimes it was: "I have major problems." And most often it was: "Shut the fuck up!" I never had the chance to talk about how amazing our kids were doing, or what legal problems I was trying to fix in Beirut. He hated to talk about bills, insisting our Lebanese taxes and legal bills came out of my grocery money.

I'd witnessed his behavior for years and tried to understand why he wanted me to feel so worthless. Narcissism at work? My plate was full with raising seven kids, running two boutiques, and managing the palace. Perhaps he felt like he lost absolute control, and I was no longer following orders. This wasn't a marriage at all anymore. He tolerated me and I obeyed, fearful he would start on his yelling rampages. I didn't know how much longer I could do this. It was unfixable. But what were my options? I had married for all the right reasons: love, children, success, and happiness. Why had this marriage taken such a dark turn?

We had stopped having sex long before Patrick was born. He had shared with me that during his boarding school years he was molested by the monks and friars. All of our children were conceived by in vitro fertilization, meaning Ramon jacked-off in a private room at the doctor's office. There was no romance, no intimacy. We had a non-existent sex life. Where had the love gone?

When in Las Vegas, I slept in my own bedroom because of his severe sleep apnea. His snoring was louder than a Harley-Davidson. I would be in bed by eleven and Ramon much later. He liked watching porn channels on our one-hundred-eighty-inch Panasonic television, usually falling asleep on the sofa. I had to get up at six in the morning and turn off the big screen before my children woke up to find graphic images in the living room. Ramon didn't care. His life was complete with gambling, prostitutes, money, and greed. The last time I saw him naked was when the doctor examined his bleeding balls, surely some disease he picked up from being a great customer of Heidi Fleiss.

My world was closing in—no escape route.

Ramon insisted on making all the decisions and constantly put me down for my opinions. I'd always been one to value not only my thoughts, but also the thoughts of others. We all have the right to speak, whether right or wrong. He never respected my opinion or that of anyone else in the room, a sure sign of narcissistic behavior. He liked to surround himself with yes men, as in "Yes, Ramon, you are so smart," or "Yes, Ramon, we will do anything for you." I was always speaking my mind and it infuriated him. He thought I was ridiculing him in front of others. His throwback was to accuse me of having a backwoods' mentality and then dismiss me in public. Remember, he was educated at the Sorbonne, and I went to modeling school. My opinions were without merit.

I found it easier to live with my kids away from the screaming and debauchery. Lebanon was a long way off from Vegas, a twenty-four-hour plane journey. Life was easier when my kids and I were living overseas where I could raise them without interference or opposition. Our lives there were full of laughter and positive notes. When in his presence life became negative, full of dark moody swings, making the simple things impossible.

With his gambling addiction, he preferred his life in Las Vegas away from the obligations of marriage. No one would witness how much money he was losing at the tables. No one would witness him flirting with so many women, spending evenings locked away in his penthouse suite. Unknowingly, over time I had become a hindrance, a liability. I grew further and further away from the fantasy of being together, knowing I was an inconvenient woman.

He had me surrounded continually with guards and chauffeurs that reported to him directly. My every move was communicated to him: where I went, whom I saw, even who I spoke to on the phone. He didn't trust anyone. I never understood what he was trying to find out, as I was married to him and living in the country of his birth. I didn't dare cheat on him, fearful of ending up in a Syrian prison for committing adultery if I even kissed the wrong man goodbye.

I played this charade for several years, flying back and forth between two countries and listening to so many rumors about his girlfriends.

Summer was approaching, and we would all be in the US for a month. The girls were enrolled in a two-week summer camp in Los Angeles while at the same time I would be taking Patrick to Culver Academy in Indiana, meaning I would be at our Las Vegas home by myself for a week.

I was all alone at the house when Ramon called me to go into his office and retrieve a fax he needed. The machine wasn't working, so I turned it off, then on again—that was the extent of my technical troubleshooting. The machine whirred to life, ejecting a document. It was a love letter written on Father's Day from the pole dancer, Tara, proclaiming her love for Ramon. She found her true soulmate and was gushing with admiration, changing her life. They've been having an affair for a year. Devastation. Realization.

Nervously I made copies, terrified he was watching me on closed circuit TV, sure his employees would come rushing into the house and confiscate the material. I felt like a government spy, if caught, shot on sight. I drove to Ramon's office, closed the office door, and said, "What's this?"

He took it from my hand and put it in the shredder, glaring at me and making all the expected excuses. I was furious. A gold digger pole dancer manipulated her way into Christian Louboutin and Herve Leger, while photos of my children were displayed on the wall above.

I had heard the rumors about his girlfriends and had looked the other way for years, knowing we were headed for divorce sooner or later. I was disgusted at his neglecting such fabulous kids and stringing me along if divorce was already in his thoughts. We discussed if we should part ways, he was willing to discuss a divorce. But I knew Ramon too well, and if I replied yes, he would have me arrested when landing back in Beirut. I still needed cash and lots of it, to fight for my kids and my future.

With him already having an army of lawyers, including Robert Shapiro, it would be the battle of my life. I was too afraid to jump. Instead, I replied, "I will just act like any wife that's been cheated on, so offer me a gift." He gave me one hundred fifty thousand dollars in cash and the conversation was over. If I had been a bit more devious, or computer savvy at this time, I would have discovered he closed escrow on a house for Tara, in Las Vegas. The purchase price was four hundred and twenty-seven thousand dollars. I would not find this out for a year, when my kids googled their dad and discovered it online.

I could live with his lies, cheating, and erectile dysfunction, but not the constant screaming. When he had problems, he took it out on me with every four-letter word in the book. Then he started in on the kids, calling my youngest, Tiffany, a "fucking midget." He screamed at them, "If you don't respect me, I will hit you so hard your head will spin!" They still remember his threats to "hang them from the chandelier." He would drive them to tears. They learned to stay in their bedrooms and watch TV until I could get them out of the house.

Patrick desperately wanted to be closer to his father and to please this man he barely knew. Ramon was taking him for rides in the Rolls Royce and teaching him how to vape. My son was learning from his father how to disrespect women, putting us in our place. At nine years old he was becoming a bully and having real anger issues. The right thing, the only thing left to do, was to get us out of this environment.

I was ready for a divorce, but this would mean a big fight for all of us.

We might lose the house, our money, and the country we called home. I would need the support of my children. They shared with me stories of how they were verbally abused by their father and how scared they had been when he was yelling at me. They were aware of his physical abuse toward me and had seen the bruises and broken furniture from his rants. They were disgusted at how he wanted all of us to be friendly with Tara and her kids, wondering why he was buying so many toys for her son and a new Bentley for her.

I was ashamed I was still married to this man. I was setting a horrible example for my children on what constitutes a healthy marriage. I was putting up with verbal and physical abuse and allowing him to scream at our children. Would he start physically abusing them? Anything was possible at this point.

I was showing my kids it was okay to choose money and things over happiness and love. Would they repeat my patterns? Would they follow in my footsteps and marry the same kind of person accepting abuse as normal?

I had been raising them with wealth and affluence, thinking that's what I wanted and needed in my childhood. In this marriage money had not bought happiness. The price had been too heavy.

It was my duty as a mom to get us back on the right track. Love and goodwill before anything. I needed to teach them independence and self-worth.

I couldn't accomplish this with Ramon. He was on a path of self-destruction.

It was my responsibility to take the lead and create a new future.

It's never too late to start, again.

Never.

Chapter Twenty-Six
Kickbacks and Tire Kicking

My kids were now teaching me about Google search, but I was not too savvy. They were researching all the scams their father was involved in. There were lawsuits from companies selling Ramon merchandise that was diverted back to gray market distributors nationwide. Companies like Matrix, L'Oreal, Clinique, and Clarins were discovering their product was selling at heavy discounts in stores like Rite Aid or CVS Pharmacy and not at the casinos as agreed upon. Large kickbacks had been paid to top executives for the product to be diverted and sold to secondary markets, readying for mass discounting. Illegal.

My girls discovered the real estate transaction where Ramon purchased Tara a home. Looking up the address, Google maps showed Ramon's car parked outside next to her new Bentley in the driveway. We found advertisements for DeSage Chocolates taken with scantily clad models draped seductively across the bed in our master bedroom. And last but not least, we found photos of parties taken in our backyard with Ramon posing in the midst of dozens of showgirls. I'd run out of excuses. It was time to lay the groundwork for a divorce.

Family meetings were a common occurrence between me and my children. Seven voices and opinions to my singular voice. We were a democracy and every voice mattered. Votes were taken on everything from what restaurant to go to or how to spend a weekend. With seven kids, each one having control of the TV remote for a day of the week. Jacky is the oldest, so her day was Monday. Patrick was lucky, having all day Sunday. I held veto power if sensing a battle coming on. We could talk at the kitchen table or in comfy chairs in their playroom, but respect was mandatory.

This family meeting was different because we knew our lifestyle was in the crosshairs. I needed the kids on board if I was going to take the path of divorce. We spoke of losing everything and moving to a new country. Leaving Lebanon was a probability, but we could find a new home in Paris or California.

"Mom, if we have to, we will all get in a van and drive to China!"

It was the final statement. We were going for it. United as a family and it was now time to start this uphill battle. I felt like I was about to enter a dark tunnel full of evil, and I was praying the light at the end would be near.

Patrick turned ten and the oldest girls turned fourteen and entering high school. They loved their school in Lebanon but were yearning to experience high school with new friends and in a positive environment away from the fear they felt with their dad. I would be turning fifty-eight in a few weeks and still had the energy to fight this battle. If I waited, I might end up seventy, with my children away at college, and me living alone in my gilded prison.

Would he take the kids? Could I get a fair settlement? Would he give me any money at all? Would he have me kidnapped, or even killed? Did I have enough money for lawyers? So many questions raced through my head, fear and panic in every thought. The tricky part was I was under constant surveillance and had to proceed very, very, carefully.

It was a stupid little thing that finally pushed me over the edge.

Christmas was coming and Ramon purchased a new Phantom Rolls Royce and a new Rolls Royce drophead convertible, probably totaling one million dollars, from his favorite dealership in Las Vegas. His new Bentley was at the warehouse, and his new Range Rover was collecting dust in our garage. And another Bentley he purchased for Tara was also sitting in our garage.

It was early December 2010, and Ramon was offering me a new car for Christmas/birthday. I was driving a 2004 GMC Yukon in

Beirut and had been looking at a larger Cadillac Escalade. Apparently, Ramon won a bundle, telling me to go to the dealer in Beirut and pick out a new car.

The funds would be wired the next day, and he was so sorry but he couldn't see us this Christmas. I guess my decision to shut up and sit in corners worked. Maybe he broke up with Tara. It didn't matter either way. I was getting a new car.

The following day I drove to the dealership in Beirut, excited to choose a new Cadillac. An Escalade in the US may have been sixty-five thousand dollars, but in Lebanon there's a thirty percent duty, putting the purchase price at one hundred thousand dollars. I gave them twenty-five thousand dollars down and made arrangements to return the next day with the remainder and pick up my car. I called Ramon to thank him for his generous gift, feeling he was making an effort. "Fuck you!" he screamed. "Who told you to buy a new car! You fucking thief! Do you think I am made of money? What the fuck do you think you are doing?" Of course, I reminded him he gifted me a new car, and I ordered it as instructed.

By then I was in tears and he was raging.

I told him, "I can live with the fact I'm in a village far away. I can put up with your gambling, your business problems, and even your girlfriends. But I cannot put up with the constant screaming at the top of your lungs. I don't want to be married to you anymore. I want a divorce."

He replied, "Don't be stupid, you know what I will do to you. I will take the kids and put you on the street. You are living in Lebanon and you have no rights. So shut the fuck up!"

We talked for the next few days. He was calming down. Now obligated to purchase the new car without his assistance, it put a strain on my bank account. I was thinking, hoping, a divorce would help us stay friends. I truly had no problem with his girlfriend Tara, if it would keep him in a better mood. He was not willing to discuss anything, and I was scared.

I had to be very careful.

Chapter Twenty-Seven
Barbarians at the Gate

My mother's health in Seattle took a turn for the worse, and I booked a ticket to the States. She'd suffered a stroke and I needed to see her. When I arrived in Seattle, her condition was worse than I imagined, placing her in a nursing home. Thank God, my two sisters helped with all the arrangements. Over the following week and after much soul searching, I thought I had the courage to move ahead and start proceedings. I was leaning on my sisters to either encourage me to get divorced, or talk me out of it.

I was terrified of Ramon and at the moment not in the same country as my children, and I used my sister's computer to search for divorce lawyers in Nevada. The best was Jim Jimmerson. I tried to book an appointment using a fake name, but he was out of town, and I took down the phone numbers of six others. I could not call any of them directly, because they might already be connected to Ramon. Las Vegas was a small community and they might alert my husband I was looking for a lawyer. He had so many attorneys for so many issues and I was not aware who may have a conflict of interest.

I caught a flight from Seattle the morning of December 13, 2010, arriving at Las Vegas Airport before nine in the morning. I called four lawyers from the airport. One, sensing my urgency, agreed to meet me at ten that morning.

Three lawyers surrounding a conference table were listening to my story, when my phone rang. The caller ID said: Mother. I answered it, fearing for the worst. Instead, it was Ramon. I put the phone on speaker so all the attorneys could listen to Ramon screaming.

"You fucking whore! I know you are in Vegas and you called Jimmerson! Are you going to serve me with divorce papers? Just wait and see what I will do!"

Ramon had bugged my phone, but I didn't know he'd hacked into my caller ID.

Immediately I filed a restraining order against Ramon for verbal abuse and filed the divorce papers. I filed in Nevada because this was where we married. I was a US citizen and community property laws were in effect. I was hoping to get a fair divorce and a fair settlement, having been married twenty years and seven children together. Even though he was cheating on me, gambling our life away, I wanted to start a new life. He could keep the girlfriend(s) and visit the kids anytime. Even at this stage I kept hoping we could rekindle our friendship, be civil, and start new lives as parents raising our kids. I didn't want a fight, I wanted freedom. I wasn't angry. We grew apart. Shit happens.

As soon as the papers were filed, I was back on a plane to Lebanon to see what he may have done. Anything was possible in the twenty-four hours it took me to travel halfway around the world. It seemed like only minutes since I had arrived back at the palace when my phone rang. It was my bodyguard. The police were at my door with papers. Should I run and hide, or see what they wanted? Every moment, every breath reminded me I was in a battle for freedom. I didn't want to lose my kids or the life I created in a foreign land, knowing my husband was capable of anything, and now he would be lashing all his fury directly at me.

My fear of barbarians at the gate was coming true. The police delivered papers from Ramon, serving me for divorce in Lebanon. As a matter of law, I filed first in America and that should stop all similar lawsuits worldwide. But what's the law have to do with it? This was Lebanon and I still had to defend myself or lose everything by default. During one of the last conversations with Ramon he threatened to use Robert Shapiro as his divorce lawyer, making my life hell. At the moment my life was hell, with or without Robert Shapiro.

My case in America progressed at a snail's pace. Ramon was refusing to accept service of any legal documents. I discovered that a process server is not allowed inside a casino in Nevada. Convenient. It was bad for business. Ramon tactfully moved into one of his penthouse suites, continuing his daily routine of losing money at the tables, while avoiding the divorce papers. I spent my days researching documents to submit to the Nevada courts and racking-up huge attorney bills. Five hundred dollars per hour. Ouch! My nights were consumed by hour-long phone calls with my attorney in Vegas on account of the ten-hour time difference. Trying to keep my kids from crying was the most difficult. They were afraid the police were going to come and take them away.

Ramon immediately stopped all payments for running the house. There was no money for food, gasoline, electricity. Remember, we were living in a palace fully staffed with guards, nannies, drivers, and huge expenses for upkeep. I started to trim the overhead by firing everyone I could, forced to pay severance wages. I had to fire all the guards and get a remote control for the gate. I'd never opened my gate on my own in the past fifteen years. Why hadn't I thought of this before? I sent most of the nannies away, and reduced my large staff of gardeners to only one. It still wasn't enough.

I put timers on the hot water, allowing my kids to shower only between six o'clock and eight o'clock in the mornings or evenings. I shut down the elevators. My expenses dropped from thirty thousand dollars per month to five thousand dollars to run the palace. This did not include food or gas, more expenses. Ramon froze all our assets. I was not allowed to liquidate cars, antiques, or property. Everything was inventoried. The bow on his legal maneuvering was to freeze my children's passports, holding them captive in Lebanon, until I divorced him on his terms. How was I going to survive?

I only had my fur coats to sell. It wasn't close to enough.

I'd keep trying.

I was finally granted a notice of default against Ramon in Las Vegas and the filings and counter-filings increased dramatically. My attorney attempted to get me money for support, but Ramon's ability to forge documents was uncanny. He produced invoices showing I purchased items for my boutique, owing him three million dollars. He introduced to the court quit claim deeds with my forged signature showing I had no interest in any US assets and even quit claiming my legal interest in our house to Tara. The judge knew he was lying, but it was another delay tactic. My resources were finite.

He wanted me to run out of money. That was the game.

After every court appearance I walked away stunned at the false evidence submitted. How could I set the record straight? The US court system was willing to examine evidence submitted as forgery, but the Lebanese courts didn't care. It was simply my word against Sheik Ramon's. With every lie or false paper filed, more filings and counter filings ensued. In no time, seventeen lawsuits were bouncing back and forth between us. An army of lawyers billing by the hour.

Even more upsetting was the fact I had to leave my kids in Lebanon while I was halfway around the world fighting for our freedom. I was terrified they would be kidnapped. Finally, the Lebanese courts granted temporary residency rights for my kids to remain in the home they grew up in. We could stay in our palace. I was appreciative the local police knew what was going on, never trying to storm the house and grab the kids. The ten-hour time difference meant I was waking at three every morning to talk to my attorneys overseas and send them urgent documents they needed. I was exhausted.

Ramon filed for divorce in Lebanon, so we tried to throw out the Lebanese case. I was fighting the same battle in two separate countries, with two sets of lawyers and different laws. Lebanon remained a man's country without equal rights for women, and the case moved forward. I couldn't ignore the case. If I did, I would be held in default and lose. If I lost, I would end up on the street with my children remanded to their fathers' brothers. As a wife and a mother, the laws were clear: I had none.

Ramon placed a travel ban on my children, which would remain in effect until they reached the age of eighteen. He was living in America and refusing to let the kids leave Lebanon. The kids cried, knowing they were stuck in the village. The US Embassy could not help us. Having dual passports had advantages and disadvantages. Living in Lebanon, we were under the jurisdiction of Lebanese law. Losing everything was a real possibility.

The light was diming.

Ramon started filing multiple lawsuits against me in Lebanon. Theft was at the top of the list and then adultery. He filed a lawsuit accusing me of having parties and entertaining men in his marital home. This was a very dangerous charge in Lebanon, carrying a mandatory prison sentence of not less than three years. He paid members of his entourage to swear they saw me having sex with men in my own home. A warrant for my arrest was issued, forcing me to report to the police station to file an affidavit denying the charges.

The officer knew me and kept apologizing for this formality, even helping me with the wording. My reputation was spotless. Living with my neighbors for twenty years, I knew the source of the complaint.

I was astounded that a father would go so far.

The gilded cage was crumbling.

Breathe.

Chapter Twenty-Eight
Law and Order?

I had filed first in Nevada to take advantage of community property laws, then Ramon filed against me in Lebanon. It was two battles in two countries with two sets of attorneys and enormous legal bills, with each team wanting to know what the other country was doing. I think there were so many documents filed that the judges in both countries couldn't and didn't even try to read them all. There were at least five-hundred pages of accusations, supporting filings, then counter-filings, and so many of the proofs were forged. How was this justice?

The court in Lebanon was in Tripoli, a tiny one room chamber where everyone was speaking Arabic. How did I end up here to fight the battle of my life? The judge was a woman and her two female assistants were notating all the happenings of the court. When the attorneys were discussing my case with the judge, I had no idea of what was going on. It was impossible to defend myself and I felt totally lost. The courtroom was old, filthy, and bustling with men shouting in Arabic.

Lebanon is a man's world and this girl from Seattle was fighting for money, custody, and freedom. There were no equal rights here.

The system was geared to have me walk out the door with nothing. How could I let this happen to myself and my kids? Whatever was to be decided by the Lebanese courts would immediately be reported to the US courts and used against me. The translations are always favoring the winner of the case. In Lebanon it was men who were pressing their thumb on the scales of justice.

My court dates having to be meticulously planned was an added hurdle to navigate when trying my case in Lebanon. My whereabouts were being tracked by my husband and his team and conveniently a car accident could impede my ability to show up. This necessitated taking different routes every time my court date came up. If I didn't show up, Ramon had everything to gain, winning the kids and getting me out of his life. The rules of the game were weighted in his favor and could easily be rearranged for the desired outcome.

I was afraid for my life, afraid for the future of my children. I had pissed him off by filing for divorce and was now terrified he would have me killed—conveniently an easy way out. His servants and bodyguards were watching my every move until I fired them all. I had no one to turn to, no one to trust. Alone.

The immediate Abi-Rached family consisted of two brothers and one sister living in Lebanon. His sister, Colette was always distant to me and I was sure she hated me. She reached out to me not long after filing for divorce to extend her blessing and wish me well. She was angry with Ramon and disgusted with the way he treated people, always using and abusing everyone.

His brothers were firmly in Ramon's court. The family grew up middle class with nannies, chauffeurs, and maids. The brothers would treat the servants like animals, screaming orders, denying food, making them sleep on the floor. It was appalling how the brothers treated the people serving them in their homes.

The feeling of superiority infiltrated other aspects of their lives, like using money as a weapon. I watched them pay bills with a flamboyant gesture of throwing cash into the air and laughing as the poor man who deserved the cash would have to scramble to the floor. It was disgusting. Ramon's brothers continually disrupted our marriage since arriving in Lebanon, reporting to Ramon that I had boyfriends and was stealing money. They became my biggest adversaries. The three brothers formed an endless web of oppression and I felt like I was divorcing the three of them. At every court proceeding in Lebanon, I had to face the two brothers representing Ramon and their wrath against me for divorcing their brother.

My legal proceedings were costing me a fortune. I was running out of money. The legal bills alone were approaching half a million dollars. If I was unable to pay my attorneys, I would lose everything by default. Ramon filed false documents stating he was only making seven thousand dollars per month. I had no access to his bank accounts, and he hid all his assets under countless LLCs.

The court proceedings in Nevada were another circus. Ramon filed a financial disclosure statement that his business and gambling debts amounted to nearly one hundred million dollars, that our property in Lebanon was worth pennies on the dollar. We had over three hundred properties in our village. I hoped one day these would go to our children. Ramon was hiding it all and was intent on keeping everything.

My name was forged on every asset in the US, giving my portion to Ramon. What was there to win? After the forgery, he mortgaged the assets to the hilt and then gambled away the money. Why even file another lawsuit? From what we could tell this was all that was left: the palace in Lebanon, some shopping centers, apartments, and vast land holdings. I wanted out. I was willing to settle for far less than I deserved. Ramon refused the offer. His strategy was to exhaust my resources with delay after delay, until I begged for a divorce on his terms.

In Nevada, Ramon was ordered during the discovery process to disclose what liens or lawsuits he was involved in, forcing him to submit a document to the family court showing he was being investigated by the criminal division of the Internal Revenue Service. I wasn't shocked. He was probably scamming on his taxes. I'd never seen any tax filings or signed any papers regarding money during our marriage. I was lucky in that regard.

At another court appearance in Nevada, I was contacted by the FBI who put me in contact with the investigating agents at the IRS. I had nothing to hide and was happy to meet with them. We arranged a meeting in Las Vegas at a secret location. During the meeting I was warned to be very careful, that my husband was considered a very dangerous man. I was aware of his capabilities in Lebanon. It was unnerving that the authorities were telling me he posed the same threat to my safety in the United States. They wanted another meeting.

Shannon was joining me to meet the IRS agents. I needed her love and support, my only confidant. We wore wigs when landing at McCarran Airport, along with large Jackie O style sunglasses. We met up with three agents from the IRS criminal division who immediately handed me a subpoena. I was now obliged to testify in their grand jury investigation regarding Ramon A. DeSage AKA Raymond Antoine Abi-Rached vs. the United States of America.

They asked me questions over a three-hour period, inquisitive and unemotional, looking for facts. I was questioned about seeing the numerous investors over the years and the circumstances revolving around the forgeries. They even asked me what I knew about Tara.

The last question they asked: Was I aware or did I have any knowledge of Ramon operating a multi-million-dollar Ponzi scheme?

Chapter Twenty-Nine
Far and Away

Did I know anything? I had no idea if I did or not.

What I did know is that he knew how to manufacture a scam. He was creative, smart, and deceptive.

I also knew he used other people's money to finance his scams.

The IRS agents asked me a million questions, never offering any information. They inquired about names, places, dates. About my life with Ramon. All I can say is I cooperated. It was the right thing to do. I was truthful while cautious, not wanting to unknowingly be involved in his criminal activities. I'd read about Bernie Madoff, the biggest Ponzi scam in history involving billions of dollars stolen from his investors. I had no idea how much money Ramon actually stole.

I'm not sure if I helped them or not. I assumed Ramon had a couple of big-time investors and through his financial disclosure he filed in our court proceedings, it showed he was down one hundred million dollars. During our marriage his finances had always been up or down in the millions, always banking on tomorrow, rolling the dice. Double or nothing, on and off the casino floor.

Ramon was always waiting for that one big break that would solve all his problems, gambling every night to keep the show going. His losses kept mounting. I tried to make the puzzle pieces fit together in my head. Who was this man? My twenty-year marriage was a complete mystery. For all I knew he could be the chess master playing us all and have fifty million dollars stashed in a bank somewhere. Or he could be in debt for the same amount, running from his fraud.

I wanted desperately to get away from this man and his wheeling and dealing. Even if he had a fortune stashed somewhere, it would take me years of litigation to discover where it was and millions in attorney fees to claw back my share. By that time nothing would be left. I wanted to sever ties and move on with my life, my children deserved better. No matter what, I needed to get away with a clean record, cutting all ties to a man facing criminal charges. The judges in both countries denied me support of any kind. My bank account was nearly empty. I was forced to start selling jewelry and furniture at pennies on the dollar to survive. Even the antiques I loved were going out the door to keep the lights on. Literally. During the winter months my saving grace was that the fur boutiques were generating enough cash to pay my attorneys. Soon the seasons would change, and with it my luck.

We were making it, barely. Day by day.

The worst part was trying to still be a mom. Ramon refused to allow the children to leave Lebanon. Christmas passed, then Easter, then the entire summer. It was his way of controlling the situation. We tried to make the best of it by visiting the mountains, the beaches, and going on picnics. I constantly worried about our safety, no longer having guards and security. I reminded myself over and over to not cry, to keep fighting. All this would end soon. I needed to be strong and responsible for my kids, who deserved a better future.

Prior to filing for divorce, I called my husband twice a day, both morning and evening. I always asked if he wanted to speak with the kids and more often than not, he was too busy. His gesture was to leave Sundays open to give the family five or ten minutes to say hello. He never knew their voices so sometimes the kids would play a game where one of them would declare they were someone else. Even their friends got in on this little game and spoke to Ramon. "Hi, Daddy!" He never knew the difference.

As soon as I filed for divorce, it became apparent Ramon was instructed by his attorney to keep a record of his phone calls to his children. He now called daily, always asking the kids if they missed their daddy and loved him. He didn't ask how they were and what was going on in their lives. Collectively the children were upset by the travel ban and would ask him why? His only reply: "It's your mother that brought this on, and only she can remove it!" The phone calls would escalate into arguments, and the kids would point out he was lying. His response was to threaten them with the travel ban. Unless they started to show some love and respect the ban would never be lifted. It was difficult to respect someone they hardly knew.

After returning to Lebanon from a court appearance in Las Vegas, Patrick approached me saying, "Mom, Dad lost it and we recorded it." I listened to over an hour of his screaming at his kids. He told them I had been a prostitute when he married me and considered me no better than their Filipino nanny. The kids wanted me to submit this to the court because they didn't ever want to live with him. My heart was breaking.

I couldn't live like this anymore. I was winning in court, but it could take years to resolve. He didn't want to give me anything. The documents he filed in court filled an entire room at my attorney's office in Las Vegas. My attorney had never seen anything like it. The documents were needless claims and counterclaims and over one hundred thousand pages of signed casino markers from his gambling. I was still working with the IRS and was required to share all of this with them. The IRS had never seen anything like it either.

The oldest twins were now approaching sixteen and wanted a new life. We were starting to hate Lebanon. It was no longer home. The hope of America was now our focus. The investigators in Ramon's criminal case were calling me frequently and warning me to be cautious. They were concerned he had put a hit on me, would kidnap the kids. The detectives in the United States saw me living in a corrupt third world country with no laws for protection. I realized time and freedom were more precious than money. I need to settle. Soon.

My attorney in Las Vegas and I agreed on a settlement that would permit me to move to California with all the kids. I would be evicted from the Palace and not allowed to take any furniture or art. I would not be given a car or money for the kid's schools. In effect, I could walk out of my marital home with my kids and my clothes. I would be given minimal child support, until they reached eighteen, and enough alimony to rent a home. He threw in a few pieces of land in our village that I would have to sell and pay US taxes. He claimed he had no US assets, therefore, there were none to divide. All of the court proceedings cost me one million dollars and over a year of fear and fighting.

Did he win? Winning is in the eye of the beholder.

It was now early 2012 and we would be going to California. My chains would be off, free to raise my kids without abuse and out of the dark cloud of my marriage. I signed this unfair agreement to escape. Freedom.

What it was not, was to get out of jail free.

After signing the agreement, he lifted the travel ban. I was worried he would impose it again. After all, who can you trust? I tested the waters, taking the kids to Italy for an Easter vacation in Rome. Coming in on approach on Easter morning our pilot circled the Vatican and I could see from my window the million worshippers in Vatican Square. We were so close I could see the Pope dressed in white on his Papal terrace, blessing all those beneath him. It was a magical moment, and I felt personally blessed to be with my children outside the world of litigation and fear.

After our vacation we returned to Beirut to pack up our life's belongings. We were going to Beverly Hills, California. To my old stomping grounds. The kids would be attending public school. They were looking forward to joining activities and sports. Lebanon had given them academics and languages and they were ready for surfing.

The girls were so excited to imagine a new home away from the shadow of the fear they saw their mom living in. They used to see me so happy and outgoing, forever the optimist. I grew into a woman on the defense, fearful of losing her kids and her life. What happened to that girl from Seattle always living in those stilettos? I want my girls to have a life of freedom and individuality.

I knew I made the right decision, leaving the opulence of palace life for a real life of family and freedom. Raising my children with real values and guiding them to independence and self-worth. It was time to get them out and let them grow up in America. I was making the right decision, even if I lost everything.

Chapter Thirty
Evicted

The land in my settlement was worthless, and I was unable to sell even one lot. I scrapped my plans to buy a home and started looking for one to rent. Buying a home brought other unwanted possibilities like being sued by one of Ramon's victims. Again, it would be a way to put me on the street. I'd been married for twenty years to a man while having no idea the depth of his deceit. I was making a new life in a new country and my first awakening was that this was going to cost a lot more than I imagined.

I had seven kids, so I needed a big house, a big car—no nannies and I'm the driver. I had to pay off the attorneys first, then put a huge deposit on a home I found near their school. With free schooling in Beverly Hills, I would not have to pay for expensive private school tuition. I rationalized the big rent and signed the lease. We were moving to Beverly Hills. Mickey Rourke was our next-door neighbor and Rodeo Drive was one hundred feet away. According to the settlement, we needed to be out of the palace the first week in July. Time to pack.

Everything in the house was already inventoried. I was not allowed to take a chair or my photos. I was forbidden to take anything that was included in a hundred-page photographed document, a court order. All I was allowed to pack were our clothes and a few items that didn't make it to the court document. I was walking away from all the memories. We were ordered to leave Lebanon on the morning of July 1st, 2012. On the day of our departure, Ramon's two brothers arrived along with the court appraiser to verify all inventory was accounted for. It took the entire day. I watched them count my China, collectables, furniture, paintings, art, and kitchen utensils.

It took me twenty years to build this home. I'd imagined a house full of kids and a happy marriage. I knew every inch of concrete and had planted every tree. My dogs in heaven are buried in the garden and my children's photo albums lined the shelves. I'd built memories, raised kids, but happy times had faded long ago. I'd spent years building relationships in this tiny village, making friends with the monks who pressed my olives between 100-hundred-year-old stones. I'd frequently visited the convent in another neighboring village to donate little girl clothes from my daughters and household items I no longer needed.

On so many mornings when the young men were out shooting the beautiful birds flying over, I would run out with fresh chicken to stop the shooting. I would miss the villagers bringing me their abandoned dogs that I would feed and care for until we found them homes. There was no humane society in the country, and I'd had the reputation of taking any and all dogs, at one time having seventeen at our home. I would miss my favorite cafe on the beach and the little chapel attached to the palace. I would miss being called Sheika. I would miss the village and the uniqueness of the country. I would miss my friends, from the wife of a Hezbollah leader to the fisherman in the bay. I would miss them all deeply.

No longer would I attend concerts under the stars at Baalbek in the breathtaking Temple of Bacchus listening to the visiting Viennese Symphony. No longer would I share a dinner with my children at the simple Chez Maggie on the beach in Batroun, feasting on the tiny fish. I would never again fall asleep in my beautiful bedroom in Chateau St. Antoine while listening to the drumbeats of the Bedouins coming down from the mountains.

I was no longer able to create any more spectacular furniture with Naji. No longer would I be serenaded by Artie and the sounds of his hand carved violin. My dreams of this palace becoming a legacy to be passed onto future generations was gone. All my hopes of living as a family were lost. Greed won. Deceit won.

I sat in the main salon as the court appraiser completed his inventory. Everything was in place. Nothing was stolen. I would not be sued. I signed, they signed, and was handed a check for twenty-five thousand dollars. My first payment of alimony. I took the check and wondered if I would ever receive another.

With all the formalities completed we were escorted out of the house and away from the world we knew, knowing we would never go back. I wasn't sad or heartbroken to leave. I had enjoyed living in this fabulous palace for twenty years. Ramon chose Caesar's Palace instead. He was the King of Las Vegas, a whale in the desert. I was a girl from Seattle who realized her childhood dream of living in a palace. A Queen of Hearts. I was the lucky one.

We packed ourselves into our cars and rented a van for our thirty suitcases. We were taking two of our dogs on the flight and found homes for all the others. I was so nervous on the one-hour drive to the airport, fearing I could still be arrested on some frivolous charge, delaying our trip and putting us in danger with no home to return to. My attorney was checking with security at the airport, making sure there were no arrest warrants for me. I didn't need a surprise. We arrived at the airport as my attorney called again to say all was clear. The eight of us proceeded to security, our passports were stamped, and we made our way to the gate.

I was asked by one of the IRS agents to call when we were safe to leave. I made the call. We were ready to board. They wished me a safe journey and promising to track my flight, and would follow-up once I arrived in Los Angeles. I reserved eight seats in the business class section. Our small dogs were beneath the seats. I was still afraid the police would arrive to take me off the plane. I looked out the window, checking to see if there were police cars chasing us. The plane taxied down the runway and took off toward Paris. Wheels up. All eight of us burst into tears.

It was always a long flight from Beirut to Paris, then Paris to Los Angeles, normally it took twenty hours. This one seemed to take forever.

We talked about our new life waiting for us in Beverly Hills. We were going to California, to a land of surfers and soccer. The children were so excited and looking forward to a new adventure.

I would show them a life of laughter and lots of friends. Our palace was so secluded that friends rarely visited. Our new home would have a new energy, a new beginning. We made it out of the glamorous prison—unchained.

I was fleeing my gilded cage with my dearest possessions, my children. The jewels of my life. Nothing else matters. Never did.

There was a new chapter to embrace. Yet the overwhelming fear of the unknown was at the foremost of my mind. I was married to one of the most notorious gamblers of all time. I knew my ex-husband would retaliate in all the ways he was so good at. Would he sue me again or should I fear for my life? Would I be held accountable for his one hundred-million-dollar Ponzi scheme? Would his victims seek me out? My inner strength had to prevail. I had the responsibility of seven children who were embarking on their own adventures. The buck began and stopped with me. I knew we would get through this, whatever lay ahead. So, the world better get ready.

We landed and cleared customs at LAX, claiming our mountain of suitcases and heading outside to our waiting airport minivans. I ordered beds online to be delivered in a couple hours to our new home in Beverly Hills.

We were all exhausted.

We would sleep in our new house tonight.

I turned on my phone and it immediately rang. It was the IRS, as they had promised to call.

"Hello, Debra, I'm glad you're in the US and safe. We wanted to let you know Ramon was arrested last night in the Bally's Casino. He was handcuffed and shackled. He is in jail awaiting a court appearance to be formally charged for wire fraud and tax evasion. Please be careful."

Epilogue

L ife is constant. We always have a beginning and an end, and can fight to begin again. We had miraculously escaped our gilded cage as a family to start fresh outside the confines of an overpowering patriarch.

As Part Two emerges we find ourselves immersed in more scandal from new litigation, cheated victims and fear of our family torn apart. Money will disappear and we will be scammed on a very personal level. Our story is so powerful, we are interviewed constantly, and the elites of Hollywood want in on it.

Slowly I open our dark curtains of privacy to a world of laughter and happiness among the children. They have a new life with California dreams and I have a chance to look for love again.

The future will bring more battles, but also a sense of calming confidence that we can't be defeated. We have lived a life of Gucci and found out the hard way that money doesn't buy happiness. Perhaps the road ahead can only be paved with optimism, gratitude, and goodwill.

Acknowledgments

I want to thank my seven children for sticking with me through thick and thin. Special thanks to my daughter Alexandra Asmar for her computer skills, and to my daughter/songwriter Jacky DeSage for her insight on putting emotion to paper. My sister Shannon Fascitelli has been my shoulder to lean on and my most loyal friend. Thanks to my collaborator Adam Francis Raby for believing in me. And special thanks to my husband Chris Hynes, who thinks everything I do is wonderful.

About the Author

Born on Christmas Day, to the name of Vallentyne, under the Chinese zodiac sign of the Dragon, Debra always knew that her destiny would be filled with fame and fantasy. Growing up in Seattle under the dark gray skies may have given her a sense of grounding, but she yearned for the footlights and a world of fashion. Discovering the glamourous cities of Paris, Milan, and Beirut, she finally settled in California. Three sets of twin girls and a son along with a best friend and sister Shannon complete a very big circle of love. She entertains frequently, visits all the best thrift shops, and enjoys music from baroque chamber to the sounds of 1970s rock and roll. Curious and positive, she now wants to share her adventures, obstacles, and life's lessons with the world. She is currently living between Beaver Creek, Colorado, and San Jaun Capistrano, California, finding happiness with her husband Chris.

Please follow Debra Vallentyne on Instagram at:
Debra_Vallentyne
and
www.DebraVallentyne.com

Made in the USA
Columbia, SC
29 September 2024

42949174R00096